Millionaire Dropouts

Also by Woody Woodward

Millionaire Dropouts High School Edition
Never Let Your Schooling
Interfere with Your Education

Millionaire Dropouts College Edition
Why Dropping Out Might Be the
Best Decision You Ever Made

Millionaire Dropouts Parents Edition
Why You Should Support Your
Child Who Wants to Drop Out

Millionaire Dropouts Biography Edition
Biographies of the World's Most
Successful Failures

Millionaire Dropouts Mini-Book:
Words of Wisdom

Millionaire Dropouts Mini-Book:
Innovators

Millionaire Dropouts

Inspiring Stories of the World's Most Successful Failures

Woody Woodward

www.MillionaireDropouts.com

© 2006 D.U. Publishing. All Rights Reserved.

Written permission must be secured from the publisher to use or reproduce any part of this book, except for brief quotations in critical reviews or articles. Request for permission or further information should be addressed to the Inspirational Product Division, D.U. Publishing.

D.U. Publishing
39252 Winchester Road #107-430
Murrieta CA 92563
admin@dupub.com
www.dupub.com

Millionaire Dropouts™ is trademark of Steven B. Woodward.

Warning—Disclaimer

The purpose of this book is to educate and inspire. This book is not intended to give advice or make promises or guarantees that anyone following the ideas, tips, suggestions, techniques or strategies will have the same results as the people listed throughout the stories contained herein. The author, publisher and distributor(s) shall have neither liability nor responsibility to anyone with respect to any loss or damage caused, or alleged to be caused, directly or indirectly, by the information contained in this book.

To preserve confidentiality, various names have been changed in this manuscript.

Some material on pages 4 and 32–33 is copyright The Oliver Press, Inc., reprinted by permission of the publisher.

ISBN-10: 0-9785802-0-6
ISBN-13: 978-0-9785802-0-9

PRINTED IN USA

Dedication

To the cynics who stopped believing in their dreams because someone once told them they couldn't do something and they believed that.

For those of us who are entrepreneurs, dreamers and builders who have always known we can. We didn't ask for permission. We made things happen by paying no attention to the critics.

Contents

- 3 **Mind Shifting**
  - 5 *Resolve to Mind Shift*
  - 11 *Letting Your Light Shine*
- 16 **Life is Unfair!**
  - 17 *Faith*
  - 18 *Family and Friends*
  - 18 *Fitness*
  - 19 *Finances*
  - 20 *Future*
- 22 **Get Off Your Assets**
  - 22 *Following Your Passions*
  - 24 *Your Passion*
- 30 **The Company You Keep**
  - 34 *Who You Listen To*
- 36 **Connecting the Dots**
- 45 **Biographical Sketches**
  - 47 *Billionaires*
    - 48 David Geffen
    - 50 H. Wayne Huizenga
    - 52 Steve Jobs
    - 54 Ray Kroc
    - 56 John D. Rockefeller Sr.
    - 58 J.R. Simplot
    - 60 Steven Spielberg

Millionaire Dropouts

- 63 *Millionaires*
  - 64 John Jacob Astor
  - 66 Andrew Carnegie
  - 68 Charles Emory Culpeper
  - 70 Del Webb
- 73 *Founders*
  - 74 Wally Amos
  - 76 William E. Boeing
  - 78 Walt Disney
  - 80 Amadeo Giannini
  - 82 Soichiro Honda
  - 84 Marcus Loew
  - 86 Joseph Pulitzer
  - 88 Sir Frederick Henry Royce
  - 90 Rick Rubin
  - 92 Harland Sanders
  - 94 David Sarnoff
  - 96 Vidal Sassoon
  - 98 Dave Thomas
  - 100 Kemmons Wilson
- 103 *Inventors*
  - 104 Thomas Edison
  - 106 Florence Melton
  - 108 Earl Muntz
  - 110 Isaac Merrit Singer
  - 112 Wilbur Wright & Orville Wright

Millionaire Dropouts

- 115 *Powerful Dropouts*
  - 116 Mortimer J. Adler
  - 118 Jackie Collins
  - 120 David Copperfield
  - 122 Simon Cowell
  - 124 Dale Earnhardt
  - 126 Albert Einstein
  - 128 William Faulkner
  - 130 Tom Ford
  - 132 Laird Hamilton
  - 134 William Hanna
  - 136 Harry Houdini
  - 138 Peter Jennings
  - 140 Rosa Parks
  - 142 Sam Phillips
  - 144 Will Rogers
  - 146 Andrew Lloyd Webber
  - 148 Adolph Zukor
- 151 *Filmmakers*
  - 152 James Cameron
  - 154 Peter Jackson
  - 156 Michael Moore

159 Your Personal Biography
162 Appendix: Who's Who of Dropouts

Definition

dropout: 1. Anyone who gives up on an activity or goal. 2. Anyone who drops out of school or conventional society.

Millionaire Dropouts

Mind Shifting

I have never let my schooling interfere with my education.
—*Mark Twain*

Let's get one thing straight right now: I do not believe in motivational speaking. I do not believe you can change your life just from hearing a story that gives you warm feelings. I believe in *mind shifting*. You have a mind shift when you actually accept a new belief as the truth and live your life accordingly. For example, when you were a child your parents told you not to touch the stove because it would burn you. They tried to motivate you to make a good decision. It wasn't until you touched the stove that you underwent a mind shift to the truth that it really would burn you.

I have systematically studied the biographies of over 1,000 people and I have interviewed many others. I've captured their secrets to success and a more meaningful life in this book. If you are ready to have a mind shifting experience, then this book is for you. If you are one of those people who cower behind their intellect and assume they can't learn anything new about life, then this book is not for you and, frankly, neither is success.

What is that one story you always tell yourself that keeps you from the success you were born to have? What is that one lie that you hide behind so you really don't have to go for it? What is your excuse? No matter how successful you are, there is a story, a lie, an excuse you use. We all do. Mine used to be that I was too dumb and that I couldn't read.

In the first grade I had a mind shifting experience when my teacher told me that I couldn't read. My mind shifted and I believed her. During the fifth grade my teacher belittled me in front of the entire class, saying I was stupid and that if I didn't follow instruction I wouldn't achieve anything. My mind shifted again: I resolved never to listen to anyone again and I decided that teachers didn't know a thing. That mind shift led to my being kicked out of two middle schools and eventually dropping out of high school at 16. I was passionate about listening to my heart and not the voices of others.

Embracing your Mind Shifts

Another man had a similar experience. William Wrigley Jr., when he was 11, dropped out of elementary school and ran away from his home in Pennsylvania by jumping on freight cars to New York City. He slept in doorways and supported himself by selling newspapers. Within a year he returned home, got kicked out of school and was forced by his parents to work ten-hour shifts in his father's soap factory. By age 29, he was done working for other people; he took his wife, small family and the $32 he had saved and moved to Chicago to make a new start as an independent sales rep. Over the next several years he sold different items including soap, toiletries and chewing gum. It wasn't until he was 32 that he had any success with chewing gum. Six years later, his competitors tried to put him out of business because he would not join an illegal price-fixing cartel with them. He had had a mind shift at a young age; if he could live on the streets of New York he surely didn't need to break the law to be successful. In 1907, when Wrigley was 46, there was a serious economic depression that put most people out of business and almost forced him into bankruptcy. He made his most daring gamble by taking out a loan for $250,000, almost twice his annual sales, and putting the money into a national advertising campaign. Within one year he went from $170,000 in sales to $3 million. And, as they say, the rest is history.

My older sister, not happy about my dropping out of high school, dragged me out of bed and enrolled me in an alternative school. Forced to make up credits, I attended school from 6:00 AM to 9:00 PM. Toward the end of my senior year it was not clear that I would have enough credits or the grades to graduate. Knowing how close it was going to be and with my previous track record, my parents did not order senior pictures, cap and gown or graduation invitations. During the senior awards assembly every one of my friends received an award for either academics or sports. Fed up with being second

Mind Shifting

rate I shifted to the fact that as soon as I crossed that graduation stage all bets were off. It was my time to go for it, without limits and excuses.

Your most dramatic mind shifts come when your passion cannot coexist with your reality. When your mind shifts it does not hesitate or retract because of fear of the unknown.

After graduation my friends went to Hawaii to celebrate; I borrowed $500 from my parents and started my first business, designing and selling T-shirts. It was my time!

With my new resolve never to be the same, I moved away from home three weeks after graduation. While attending a junior college I was tested with fifth grade spelling and reading comprehension levels. Committed, I started to read insatiably. But I never overcame my original mind shift, that educators didn't know anything. I dropped out by the end of the year.

People often say, "Get a good education and then you will get a good job." But there is no standard plan for dropouts. No one says, "Go to college, spend a night in jail for a prank, drop out and you will be successful." I have paid a serious price for my choices but some prices are worth paying.

I don't care who you are or who your parents are; you do not get what you want out of life unless you create it.

Resolve to Mind Shift

If you had a mind shift so that under *no* circumstance would you quit until you succeeded, do you believe you would succeed? If you can't answer yes to that question you cannot put this book down until we get your mind to shift to the reality of the power that is within you. Abraham Lincoln said, "Always bear in mind that your own resolution to succeed is more important than any other." History has proved this point. Here is a list of companies that were started or owned by school dropouts who didn't quit until they succeeded. You may recognize a few. You may own stock in one or two. You might even work for one of them.

- American Apparel
- American Financial Group, Inc.

- Amstrad plc
- Apple Computer, Inc.
- Auntie Anne's, Inc.
- Bank of America, N.A.
- Ben & Jerry's Homemade Ice Creame
- Blockbuster Inc.
- The Boeing Company
- Cablevision Systems Corp.
- The Coca-Cola Company
- Columbia Pictures Industries, Inc.
- Def Jam Recordings
- Dell Inc.
- Dole Food Company
- Domino's Pizza L.L.C.
- Dow Jones & Company, Inc.
- The Drudge Report
- Dunkin' Donuts Incorporated
- DreamWorks SKG
- Eastman Kodak Company
- Elizabeth Arden, Inc.
- Exxon Mobil Corporation
- Famous Amos Chocolate Chip Cookie Company, L.L.C.
- Ford Motor Company
- The Gillette Company
- Grey Goose Importing Company
- The Hershey Company
- Holiday Inn
- J.R. Simplot Company
- JetBlue Airways
- Jimmy Dean Foods
- Johnson Publishing Company, Inc.
- Kaiser Aluminum
- Kentucky Fried Chicken
- Loews Theatres
- Mars Incorporated
- Max Factor
- McDonald's Corporation

- Metro-Goldwyn-Mayer Studios Inc.
- Microsoft Corporation
- Miss World Pageant
- Motown Records
- Napster, LLC
- NBC
- Netscape
- The New Yorker
- Oracle
- Polaroid Corporation
- Polo Ralph Lauren Corporation
- Proctor & Gamble
- Rolling Stone Magazine
- Rolls-Royce plc
- Success Magazine
- United Artists
- Vidal Sassoon
- Virgin Enterprises, Ltd.
- The Walt Disney Company
- Wendy's International, Inc.
- Westinghouse Electric Corporation
- Whole Foods Market
- World Marketing Alliance
- Wm. Wrigley Jr. Company
- Yahoo! Inc.

I wandered around for a couple of years before deciding that I wanted to be married before achieving financial success. I was engaged three times between October 1994 and February 1995.

The last engagement stuck; I have been married to my sweetheart for over ten years now. I met my wife on a Wednesday and we went out Friday and Saturday. By Sunday I told her I was going to marry her. She said okay and we were married within five months. It would have been sooner if her parents hadn't made us wait. I would have been married by Tuesday. When you want something more than food and oxygen, there is nothing that will keep you waiting—except in-laws.

What decisions have you made impulsively? Has there been a time when you said yes or no to something without calculating the end result? That is called living by the seat of your pants. There is no greater feeling than just going for it with reckless abandon. It makes you feel alive. Think of another time when you hesitated and, because of that hesitation, you lost the opportunity. We all have them. My story is not special. When was the last time you felt truly alive? What were you doing? Write it in the space below:

_____

_____

_____

_____

Impulsive Decisions

At his peak, Sylvester Stallone was one of the most popular and highly paid stars in Hollywood, commanding a fee of $20 million per movie. It wasn't always that way.

He was expelled from 14 schools by age 15. Growing up, he wanted to be an actor more than anything else. His wife advised him to give up his fantasy and get a normal job. He replied that by doing so would be selling out.

Stallone ended up so broke that he had to sell his dog for $50 to buy food. During these dark days he saw a fight between world heavyweight champion Muhammad Ali and Chuck Wepner, an underdog who no one thought would make it past the third round. Inspired by this match he wrote the Rocky script in 84 hours.

After being turned down countless times he got a chance to sell the script for $75,000 on one condition—he was not going to be the actor. Even though he was broke and hungry he impulsively stood his ground and declined the offer. The only way he was going to sell the script was if he was the lead actor. The company refused, offering him $250,000, then $1 million for the script with the same condition. He said no on each offer. He was hungry but was not willing to sellout on his dream. They finally gave in and offered to do the movie on a shoestring budget, giving him $35,000 as the

Mind Shifting

writer and actor; if the movie was successful he would share in the profits. He immediately agreed.

Stallone took the money and went back to the man who bought his dog. He offered $100 to buy his dog back. The man said he was not interested. Stallone offered more and more but the man still would not budge. Stallone was committed to do whatever it took to get his dog back. He eventually paid the owner $15,000 and gave him a walk-on part in Rocky.

Impulsive decisions have a cost that, even though it may be high, might be exactly what it takes to create a mind shift. Stallone made an impulsive decision to sell his dog but the fight was in him to get his dog back no matter what. It is that same fight that has made the Rocky franchise a billion dollar business. By the way, Stallone divorced his wife but paid to keep the dog.

What are your dreams worth? Better yet, what are you worth? Have you ever calculated that there are 525,600 minutes in a year? You work 120,000 of those minutes. That is almost a quarter of your year. What is that worth? I'll bet you are underpaid for your time. You are paid for the activity you perform but the actual worth of your contribution could be much greater than what you are making.

Let me prove it. When I was engaged, I took the worst advice I was ever given: "Quit being self employed and get a real job." I took a "real job" paying $7.50 an hour as a screen printer, and I was miserable. Within six months I told my new bride that I had quit my job. As I had only known this woman for less than nine months, I was not sure how she was going to take the news. Her reply was one of my greatest mind shifts and has set the pattern for the rest of our lives. She said, "It is about time. Now you can do what you really want." With that encouragement I signed up to sell juggling sticks at a local Renaissance festival.

We made $6,000 during that two-week festival. The amazing part is that we sold out of our inventory within the first three days. My supplier of juggling sticks wouldn't send me any more. A new shift set in. Was I going to rely on someone else to provide me product and dictate how much money I was going to make or was I going to do it myself? With no formal experience in manufacturing, I jumped in and worked 20 hours a day trying to figuring it out. I begged my sister and friends to help me manufacture around the clock. By the end of the festival, we had made more in two weeks than I did in five months of screen printing. That mind shift had a profitable outcome. A couple of years later, I sold the juggling business, collected royalties, traveled the country and purchased a second home. You can still purchase those juggling sticks nationwide at most major retailers. Often the effects of a mind shift are unknown until you look back years later and connect the dots of your life.

You never know what will inspire a mind shift. As a boy I saw the movie *Big*, starring Tom Hanks. Hanks worked in a toy company designing and manufacturing toys. I told myself right then and there that if someone has a job like that it might as well be me. If you throw that kind of committed desire out in the universe, I believe it comes true. The unsuccessful call it luck; the successful call it the meeting of preparation and opportunity. As opportunity would have it, a business associate was meeting with the president of a national toy company. I set out to dazzle him with my résumé of building and selling a juggling company. Keep in mind I had no graphic arts experience or college education. I asked my wife to review my résumé, and she gave me another powerful mind shift. She said "This isn't you. Do it with your style." Knowing what she meant I threw it away and ran to the toy store. I put my résumé on an Etch-a-Sketch. The shift was that companies don't want a manufactured résumé of past accomplishments. They want a person that will wow them and make them need you on their team. It was enough to get their attention. Within a week we had flown first class to their headquarters and started a new job. By letting my true personality shine, I was able to shake up a 100-year-old toy company.

Feeling stifled in my new career I had another shift. If I was working at a toy company it needed to be outrageous and fun the way toys are. I ripped the 50-year-old oak paneling off my walls, splashed paint on the wood studs and designed a new wall from foam shapes. It is easier to get forgiveness than permission, so I did it at night. I didn't realize how the wiring ran through the wall, and I caused a short that knocked out the power in the entire west wing of the building. Needing help, I called my older brother on the west coast, waking him up. I begged him to help me figure out how to get the power back on. We got the lights back on about 30 minutes before the first shift arrived. Letting your true light shine has its cost. Some people hated my remodeling job, but those who made the decisions knew what I was going for. They invited me to redo the stairway and waiting room, then flew me to New York to redesign their showroom for the International Toy Fair.

Letting Your Light Shine

Why are we so afraid of letting our true light shine? Nelson Mandela said, "There is no passion to be found playing small—in settling for a life that is less than the one you are capable of living." In her book *A Return to Love*, Marianne Williamson said:

> Our deepest fear is not that we are inadequate. Our deepest fear is that we are powerful beyond measure. It is our light, not our darkness that most frightens us. We ask ourselves, Who am I to be brilliant, gorgeous, talented, fabulous? Actually, who are you *not* to be? You are a child of God. Your playing small does not serve the world. There is nothing enlightened about shrinking so that other people won't feel insecure around you. We are all meant to shine, as children do. We were born to make manifest the glory of God that is within us. It is not just in some of us; it is in everyone. And as we let our own light shine, we unconsciously give other people permission to do the same. As we are liberated from our own fear, our presence automatically liberates others.

Letting your true light shine has its effects. Word got out about what I was doing at this toy company, and other companies started calling. The toy industry is like the mafia. It is difficult to get in but, after you are in, other members want you. Having only worked for my current employer for nine months I was flattered when Mattel, Duncan Yo-Yos and Radio Flyer called. By the tenth month I took a job at a start-up company because they offered me 35 percent more pay. Within two weeks my wife and I had moved to another city and rented an apartment in a high-rise complex. Within a week of getting settled into my new job I was fired. The company lost $1 million on a defective product that I came on board to save, and I was the first one to go after the decision was made to cancel production.

With bills stacking up and the pressure to provide, my wife and I went to our apartment manager and asked for work. We did odd jobs from cleaning toilets to spraying for roaches, trash removal and apartment repairs. It did not hit me until I was climbing into a dumpster pulling out trash from the trash compactor that this was not what I was born to do. I take great pride in work. My father and mother raised my siblings and me to have a strong work ethic. It makes no difference to me if you are a CEO or a garbage man. There is great pride in meeting your responsibilities. However, I knew I was meant for more. A new mind shift set in: I would never work for someone else again. We sold our personal belongings, packed what was left into a small U-Haul and headed west across the country to my in-laws.

Within one year we had gone from being self-employed, living in our three bedroom home to quitting a job, getting fired from another and selling almost everything we had to moving into a spare bedroom in my in-laws home.

When you make a mind shift in your life during a painful time or because of pressure, you end up with your most dramatic results. Have you ever gone from an abusive relationship to finding the person of your dreams? Have you ever gone from a horrible working environment to finding your dream job? What about the last time you stuck to your workout routine and lost the weight you wanted to? Did you ever get so disgusted with your situation that you made a committed change and created a better situation for yourself? That is a mind shift. The more pain associated with the cause of the mind shift, the longer lasting the results will be.

I was exhausted from living below what I was capable of achieving. My mind shifted; I resolved to be successful beyond any of my previous goals. Through previous contacts, I was able to partner with another associate and do contract work for the largest toy company in Canada. That contract work led to crisscrossing North America and Asia, where I set up three factories. The product we co-designed sold 200,000 units by Christmas. Knowing the benefits of royalties and ownership, we structured the deal to make money on each unit sold. Life sometimes gives you a raw deal; I

Mind Shifting

did not see any of those proceeds. The money I should have collected would have been near six figures. Time for a new shift! From then on we used an attorney to draft all agreements and we issued private stock in a company so there would be ownership.

With the success and the experience I had developed in Asia I was able to partner with two successful businessmen. One partner had just sold his business for a couple million at age 36 and was finishing his 10,000-square-foot home; the other partner had a patent on a product that we were going to market and sell. His prior sales of this product had been nearly $40 million. At the same time, he was taking another one of his companies public. I finally encircled myself with the right people. During the next two years we formed a corporation and issued private stock as well as spending nearly $1 million on product development and research. This opportunity gave me the chance to circle the globe, setting up different factories in China and Thailand. Within two years the dot-com boom was reaching its peak. As you remember, people were throwing money at any idea that would give them inside stock options. We raised over $2 million from outside investors. This valued my private stock at almost $1 million. With the value of my stock and other assets I was a millionaire at 26. Going from trash and toilet man to millionaire within two years went to my head. Most of my friends had just graduated college and were starting their careers. Here I was jet-setting across the country, riding in limousines, having the time of my life. It is strange how the universe keeps score. When you are on top of the world the world has a way of humbling you.

Being full of myself, I started disagreeing with my partners. Eventually I left the company. It didn't matter to me, because the royalties from the sale of the juggling company were starting to increase and we were able to buy a second home. Still feeling on top of the world I negotiated a buyout for my stock with my partners. Figuring I was set for a long time I started investing heavily in the stock market during 1999 and 2000. If you were investing at the same time, you know where this story is going.

I blame the entire crash of the stock market on my wife. If you lost money at that time I will let you blame her as well. My wife told me a year after we had lost everything that she prayed to make me humble. If you have never had a testimony or proof that prayer works then ask to be humbled. I guarantee that prayer will be answered.

We went from having everything to nothing in less than six months. We were losing $6,000 a day in the market as well as having my previous partners back out of my buyout because the market was affecting them as well. My private stock was valued at zero and my money in the market was slipping faster than I could control it. Eventually we sold our second home, toys, cars and anything else that would fetch a dollar. Realizing the inevitable, we rented out our home and moved into my parents' unfinished basement. We had gone from a 4,200 square-foot home with unused bedrooms to less a single bedroom of less than 140 square feet. We put all of our possessions and our six-month-old son into one bedroom of my parents' unfinished basement.

In our married life this was the darkest hour. Our son had been prescribed the wrong medication and was hospitalized. The doctor was telling us that if he lives through the night he should be okay but we wouldn't know the long-term effects. Collectors were coming at us for loans we signed when I was in business with my partners. I will never forget the day the bank called and said we only had four dollars in all of our accounts combined. We went to meet with a bankruptcy attorney and filled out the paperwork. I was a 27-year-old former millionaire filing for bankruptcy.

Once again, in your most painful experiences come your strongest mind shifts. My wife showed her truest colors and said, "If you could do anything in this world what would you do?" I took it to heart and shifted again. Since I was a little kid, I have been fascinated with all the elements of real estate. My father and I spent countless hours in my youth walking through homes on the weekends. My wife and I had bought our first home when we were 22. What I wanted more than anything else was to get my real estate license and market homes.

One thing led to another. I was able to get my real estate license in record time. I believe that, as much as the universe likes to level the playing field in your life, it also sends people into your life who at the time are like living angels to assist you. I have had a few angels in my life. One of my first angels gave me a private loan to start

Mind Shifting

the juggling company. The second angel came in a telephone call. A friend called and offered me a job marketing his 1,200-home golf and gated lakefront project. He offered to pay me $30 an hour as well as split the commission on the real estate.

This was enough to take the sting out of our monthly bills and keep us out of bankruptcy. My wife started to run a mortgage processing company from home. We didn't have the money to buy the necessary software to get it started. We put the $900 software purchase on our last credit card. When you have only four dollars in your checking account, $900 feels like a million.

We were able to get by, and over a five-year period we turned that small home-based mortgage processing and real estate company into a seven-state empire with gross sales over $30 million.

By age 32 I had learned the real meaning of what it meant to be wealthy and the true meaning of sticking to your guns and going for it.

Life is Unfair!

Life is unfair, go out and get your unfair share.
— *Todd Clarke*

Do you really believe life is unfair? Whether you do or don't, you're right. There is no convincing you otherwise. This book is full of stories of people who had an unfair life. But it will make no difference to you because your views on your own circumstances are personal. It is easy to say that Walt Disney dropped out of high school, filed bankruptcy, had his entire staff pirated from him by his competitor, had his opening day at Disneyland bomb and died of cancer before his greatest triumph, Walt Disney World, was finished. But he was successful in the end and Disneyland is still running today. It is all in your perspective.

No one other than yourself can compel you to believe that your life has been fair. Doing so would insult your past experience. At some point your life has been unfair. It may actually be so right now. Would you like to see when your life was unfair but you still excelled? To show you, I need you to list two achievements in each of what I call the five F's: faith, family and friends, fitness, finances and the future.

- **Faith** (When did you have a spiritual experience in your life?)

    1. _____

    2. _____

- **Family and friends** (When did someone convey their love for you either as a child or adult?)

    1. _____

    2. _____

Life Is Unfair

- **Fitness** (When where you happiest with your body and health?)

    1. _____

    2. _____

- **Finances** (What sparked a financial success in your life?)

    1. _____

    2. _____

- **Future** (In the past when were you so tired of how unfair life was that you swore in the future it would be different and it was?)

    1. _____

    2. _____

Looking back on your life, what caused these successes? Usually, our successes are triggered when life is either unfair or difficult. The stories below illustrate the cliché, the night is darkest before the dawn.

Faith

Have you ever been bullied? Can you recall the last time you were intimidated? Someone in your life has intimidated you; so you react differently toward them. In high school I had a bully who was relentless. He was older and bigger; his friends were bigger than my friends. There was no escaping him. When I talked to my parents about this bully, they asked me if I had prayed for help. Taking their advice I prayed for the strength to overcome my feelings when he intimidated me. A few weeks later at a party, he insulted me in front of about 40 people. My mind shifted and right then and there I decided I would never back down again from anyone. I lunged for him and challenged him in front of everyone. I had had enough. Either he or I was going to die that night. He saw the fight in my eyes and never challenged me again. I believe that my prayers were answered. I continue to pray over everything that is important to me.

Family and Friends

Would you ever say Jim Carrey's life is unfair? He is currently one of the highest paid actors in Hollywood. He commands more than $20 million a picture. It wasn't always this way. His family fell onto hard times when he was in high school. His father lost his job and the family had to move. The entire family had to work at the Titan Wheels factory. Jim worked an eight-hour shift every day after school. When the family finally quit the factory, they lived in a Volkswagen camper van for a while before moving to Toronto. These were unfair times for a high school boy struggling to find his own identity.

Carrey turned to comedy as an outlet. His first attempt to break into the comedy scene was a disaster. He performed at Yuk Yuk's, a local club, and the show did not do well. Disappointed, he spent the next two years improvising and reworking his material. When he performed again, he was a major hit.

He dropped out of high school and moved to Los Angeles in 1979. One story Carrey loves to tell everyone is how he celebrated his arrival in Hollywood in his old Toyota and with no work at hand. He wrote himself a post-dated check for ten million dollars and kept it with him as a source of inspiration. Just three days before his father's death, Carrey received $10 million dollars for The Mask. He slipped the old check he had written to himself into his dad's pocket before the coffin was closed. Carrey's life was unfair but he found the power to get past it and now he collects $20 million of his unfair share per movie.

Fitness

By the time Lance Armstrong was 17 he was cycling professionally. He went on to set world records at a young age. By 1996, at 25, he was ranked seventh in the world. His contract with the Cofidis Cycling team gave him an annual salary of $600,000.

In October 1996, he was diagnosed with testicular cancer. The doctor told him he had tumors in the abdomen, in the lungs and

Life Is Unfair

in the lymphatic nodes. His chances of survival were estimated by the specialists from 60 percent to 80 percent. Later, these numbers were revised downward to below 50 percent. Armstrong went under the scalpel. After lesions were found on the brain, his chances were once again revised downward. One of his doctors privately evaluated Armstrong's chance of survival at three percent but told Armstrong 40 percent to give him hope. Normal chemotherapy would have probably ended his cycling career because of the damage this treatment would have caused to the lungs. The doctors opted for an innovative chemotherapy offered at the Indiana University.

After his successful treatment, Armstrong went back to cycling, but his team's sponsor dropped him and ended his lucrative contract.

Armstrong didn't lose any time. He joined the Unites States Postal Service team for a third of his previous pay. From 1999 to 2005 he won seven consecutive Tours de France. In 2002, Sports Illustrated magazine named him their sportsman of the year. The Associated Press named him male athlete of the year for 2002, 2003, 2004 and 2005. He received ESPN's ESPY Award for best male Athlete in 2003, 2004 and 2005; and he won the BBC sports personality of the year overseas personality award in 2003. Armstrong retired from racing at the end of the 2005 Tour de France, but his success prompted some to nickname the event the Tour de Lance.

Not only did he go on to get his unfair share of success as a racer but his Livestrong organization has raised over $60 million for cancer research, too.

Finances

Here is a short list of people known for their success but who had to file for bankruptcy. Most of them did not become successful until they had first failed financially.

- **Samuel L. Clemens (Mark Twain)** filed in 1894
- **Walt Disney** filed in 1923
- **William Fox**, co-founder of Twentieth Century Fox Film Corporation, filed in 1936
- **Ulysses S. Grant** filed in 1884

Millionaire Dropouts

- **Larry King** filed in 1978
- **Gary Kurtz**, Producer of Star Wars and American Graffiti
- **Donald Trump** filed in 1992. At one point Donald Trump was over $900 million in debt.
- **P.T. Barnum** filed in 1871. After filing bankruptcy he decided to follow his passion, starting his circus empire.
- **Henry John Heinz** filed in 1869. After failing at two other condiment companies, he decided to work on a new condiment called ketchup.
- **Henry Ford** filed in 1903. He ran two other motor car companies into the ground before he started the Ford Motor Company.
- **Rembrandt** filed in 1656. Most of his famous works came after bankruptcy.
- **Mozart** filed in 1790.
- **Thomas Jefferson** filed in 1826.
- **L. Frank Baum**, author of The Wizard of Oz, filed in 1888. He did not write the The Wizard of Oz until after his bankruptcy.
- **Milton Hershey** failed in many businesses before he succeeded with candies.
- **Charles Goodyear** filed in the 1930s.

Future

Take whatever you currently feel is unfair and project out—a week, month or year—when you will change it. Write below the success story of what you will have done to get your "unfair share" in the future.

_____

_____

_____

_____

Life Is Unfair

Battles are not won by the strong. They are won by the determined. General George Patton said, "Most battles are won before they are ever fought." Life is nothing more than a mind game of overcoming our obstacles. When we concentrate on our future being the way we want it, the future will take care of itself. The appendix lists prominent dropouts in groups. Under the heading "Company Founders," you will recognize names from Wally Amos of Famous Amos Chocolate Chip Cookies to William Wrigley Jr. of Wrigley's Chewing Gum. These men were called visionaries. Were they really? Or did they focus so much on the future being the way they wanted it, that it became self fulfilling. Today, you have to be so determined to overcome your obstacles that the future bends to meet your expectations.

Get Off Your Assets

Your worth consists in what you are and not in what you have.
—*Thomas A. Edison*

MANY PEOPLE GO through life reacting instead of taking charge. Being famous or successful by the world's definition is unimportant. You can get so much more out of life if you tap into your own skills and assets. The majority of people are afraid to take a risk outside their comfort zone. Fear (of the unknown or of the risk) is the main thing that keeps us from achieving our potential. Think of fear as an acronym for False Evidence Appearing Real. What you fear is not the same as what another person fears. Getting off your assets means rejecting all false evidence that holds you back and tapping into what you already know or have an interest in. Did you know that most companies today were started by someone's hobby or interest? Look at Microsoft, Disney, Famous Amos, Holiday Inn, Bank of America and Domino's, for example. What if Bill Gates feared that playing with computers wouldn't be profitable or Walt Disney decided that nobody really wants to see cartoons on a big screen? Our economic landscape would not be the same if these dropouts did not take a risk to follow their passions.

Following Your Passions

Almost every good business stems from an interest or hobby. My first business started from my interest in designing.

When I was 16, I sold my first idea to a local clothing store, Above the Belt. It is now the hottest chain nationwide, with over 200 stores and a new name, Zumiez. One of the fondest memories of my youth was walking into owner Tom Campion's office and telling him I had a product he had to buy. After showing him my key chains

Get Off Your Assets

made from bicycle chains, he said yes. Then he started talking about purchase orders, invoicing and net 30. It might as well have been a foreign language; I had no idea what he was talking about. Tom took the time to educate me about the business and how it worked. He is a master marketer; in 2005 he took Zumiez public, and I am proud to say I own stock in the company that launched one of my first products and my career. Tom gave me a job at a store in the mall and invited me to help set up one of his new stores. There is no way he could ever know about the impact he had on my life, but when you follow your passion you will come in contact with other passionate people who influence you by the way they follow their passion.

One of Tom's passions is that he gives to local environmental causes, and Tom is my role model. Since I was 16, my companies have always given ten percent of their net earnings to local charities.

One of the greatest impacts you can have on your passion is to associate yourself with other people who are passionate. As I entered my twenties I built a juggling company, developed products that sell at the top five big box stores, jointly operated a company going public, traveled the world setting up factories, researched patents for new inventions and built a strong real estate and mortgage operation. You never know what your hobbies will turn into. But I guarantee that if you don't do something with those hobbies and interests you will never know the sweet feeling of success you might have had.

The simplest idea may spawn another and another until you connect with the one thing that makes you a success. While I was a teenager, my mom and a friend started a business of decorating restaurant tables with little vases full seasonal flowers. What a simple idea! They never knew what that would grow into. Fifteen years later you can go to restaurants, doctors' offices and other establishments to see their creation. She no longer runs that company and hasn't for many years, but it is still up and running. The biggest impact that business had was not on its patrons or owners but on me. I was fascinated that someone could start a company from scratch, then go out and sell products they created. It was the start of what has become an addiction for me, and that is to start businesses. My best friends and I laugh about it quite often. When we get together we always discuss each other's hobbies and interests. When I was 17 and finally graduated high school, my mom and I went down to the city building and opened my first business, called Northwest Designs; and 15 years later my greatest hobby and interest outside my family is still to start different businesses.

What if you follow your passion or interest and then fail? You wouldn't be the first or the last. What is failure? Is there really such a thing? Thomas Edison failed over 2,000 times before he invented the incandescent bulb. He would say developing that light bulb was a 2,000-step process.

Recovering from Failure

David Neelman knows the results of overcoming failure. He dropped out of college to pursue his passion as an entrepreneur. At 23, Neelman's first attempt in the business world was a discount travel business. Within a year he filed bankruptcy and was out of business. He then went to work at a travel agency to find out what he had done wrong and how to better operate his next business. The next ten years involved a lot of ups and downs. Neelman started a small discount airline in Salt Lake City. Within a couple of years, Southwest Airlines bought out his company and he was a multimillionaire. Southwest hired him but then fired him within five months.

Neelman was not deterred. In due time he started another airline, Jet Blue. For most airline companies now is not the time to expand or to start new operations. Jet Blue is not like most companies. Since its inception Jet Blue has grown rapidly. It offers discount travel on a fleet of new planes; in 2005 it was ranked first in the annual Airline Quality Ranking. Not bad for a failure and dropout.

"The future belongs to those who believe in their dreams."

—*Eleanor Roosevelt*

Your Passion

Have you ever been watching an infomercial late at night and said, "I could have thought of that," or, even worse, realized you did think of it and someone else beat you to the market? Countless times, I have been looking through a magazine or walking through a store only to see a product I was working on at my shop. We all live on this great planet and the influences that shape our own thoughts also shape those of others—at about the same time.

One of the most intriguing things about innovation is that it thrives on competition. I tire of people who say that someone already has it out there or that their product or idea will never work. When was the last time you got into your Ford Model A? Without competition we would all be driving at 15 mph on dirt roads or, even worse, still be driving a horse and buggy. Competition and innovation separates us from the animal kingdom. Without them we might as well just walk around searching and gathering food as the animals do.

What ideas have you been sitting on? It could be anything from an invention to a marketing idea for your company to starting a new business. Write them here:

_____

_____

_____

_____

What action are you going to take to follow your passion? Write it here:

_____

_____

_____

_____

Consider these great inventions that would not have been developed without someone stepping out of their comfort zone and following their passion. These were ordinary people, not corporations:

- Airbag (Allen Breed)
- Air brake (George Westinghouse)
- Air conditioning (Willis Carrier)
- Airplane (Orville and Wilbur Wright)
- Apple computer (Jobs and Wozniak)
- Avery labels (Stan Avery)
- Ballpoint pen (John Loud)
- Basketball game (James Naismith)
- Beanie Babies (Ty Warner)
- Blue jeans (Levi Strauss)
- Brown paper bag (Margaret Knight)
- Calculator (William Seward Burroughs)
- Candy Land game (Eleanor Abbott)
- CB walkie-talkie (Al Gross)
- Celestial Seasonings tea (Mo Siegel)
- Celluloid (John Hyatt)
- Clue board game (Anthony Pratt)
- Coca-Cola (Dr. John S. Pemberton)
- Corn flakes (Will Kellogg)
- Cracker Jack (F.W. Rueckheim)
- Crayola crayons (Binney & Smith)
- Curling Iron (Theora Stephens)
- Delta faucet (Alex Manoogian)
- Diesel engine (Rudolph Diesel)
- Digital fax (Robert Wernikoff)
- Digital compact disk (James Russell)
- Dishwasher (Josephine Garis Cochraine)
- Disposable diaper (Marion Donovan)
- Disposable paper cup (Hugh Moore)
- Earmuffs (Chester Greenwood)
- Electric shaver (Jacob Schick)
- Electromagnetic motor (Nicola Tesla)
- Elevator (Elisha Otis)

Get Off Your Assets

- Erector Set (A.C. Gilbert)
- Escalator (Jesse Reno)
- Etch-A-Sketch (Paul Chase)
- Fax (Elisha Gray)
- Fig Newton (James Mitchell)
- Frisbee (Fred Morrison)
- Frozen foods (Clarence Birdseye)
- Frozen pizza (Rose Totino)
- Gatling gun (Richard Gatling)
- G.I. Joe (Stanley Weston)
- Golf tee (Dr. William Lowell)
- Gore-Tex fabric (Wilbert L. Gore)
- Grocery cart (Sylvan Goldman)
- Hawaiian Tropic suntan oils (Ron Rice)
- Helicopter (Igor Sikorsky)
- Hot Wheels toy cars (Elliot Handler)
- Incandescent bulb (Thomas Edison)
- Jell-O (Peter Cooper)
- Jet ski (Clayton Jacobsen)
- Kirby vacuum (Jim Kirby)
- Kitty litter (Edward Lowe)
- Kool-Aid (Edwin Perkins)
- Koosh ball (Scott Stillinger)
- La-Z-Boy recliner (Edwin Shoemaker)
- Lear jet (Bill Lear)
- Lego toys (Ole Kirk Christiansen)
- Life Savers candy (Clarence Crane)
- Lincoln Logs (John Lloyd Wright)
- Lionel toy trains (Joshua Lionel Cowen)
- Liquid Paper (Bette Nesmith Graham)
- Matchbox toy cars (Jack Odell)
- Maytag washers (Fred Maytag)
- Miniature golf (Garnet Carter)
- Monopoly board game (Charles Barrow)
- Morse code (Samuel Morse)
- Nerf ball (Reynolds Guyer)
- Nike shoe (Bill Bowerman)

Millionaire Dropouts

- Odor-Eaters (Herbert Lapidus)
- Pepperidge Farm (Margaret Rudkin)
- Pepsi-Cola (Caleb Bradham)
- Phillips-head screw (Henry F. Phillips)
- Phonograph (Thomas Edison)
- Plastic (Leo Baekeland)
- Play-Doh (Joe McVicker)
- Polaroid camera (Edwin Land)
- Polarizing sunglasses (Edwin Land)
- Popsicles (Frank Epperson)
- Potato chips (George Crum)
- PowerBar snack food (Brian Maxwell)
- Power steering (Francis Davis)
- Radio Flyer wagon (Antonio Pasin)
- Raggedy Ann & Andy (John B. Gruelle)
- Ready-mixed paint (Henry Sherwin)
- Reel-to-reel film (Hannibal Goodwin)
- Respirator (Dr. Forrest Bird)
- Revolver (Samuel Colt)
- Rollerblades (Scott and Brennan Olsen)
- Rollercoasters (John Miller)
- Safety pin (Walter Hunt)
- Safety razor (King Gillette)
- Samsonite luggage (Jesse Shwayder)
- Scrabble board game (Alfred Butts)
- Silly Putty (Peter Hodgson)
- Slinky toy (Richard James)
- Snowblower (Arthur Sicard)
- Snowboard (Tim Sims)
- S.O.S. scouring pads (Edwin W. Cox)
- Strobe lights (Harold Edgerton)
- Submarine (Cornelius van Drebbel)
- Supercomputer (Seymour Cray)
- SuperSoaker (Lonnie Johnson)
- Tabasco Sauce (Edmund McIhenny)
- Teva sandals (Mark Thatcher)
- Telephone (Alexander Graham Bell)

- Television (Philo Farnsworth)
- Traffic light (Garrett Morgan)
- Tickle Me Elmo doll (Ron Druben)
- Timex watches (Joakim Lehmkuhl)
- Tinkertoy (Charles Pajeau)
- Tow truck (Ernest Holmes Sr.)
- Trampoline (George Nissan)
- Tupperware (Earl Tupper)
- Twister (Chuck Foley)
- Typewriter (Christopher Sholes)
- Vacuum cleaner (Ives McGaffney)
- Velcro (George de Mestral)
- Vicks VapoRub (Lunsford Richardson)
- Vulcanized rubber (Charles Goodyear)
- Walkman (Jerome Lemelson)
- Waterbed (Charlie Hall)
- Water softener (Emmett Culligan)
- Wheelchair (Harry Jennings)
- Zamboni (Frank Zamboni)
- Zipper (Whitcomb Judson)

A final thought: Alan Greenspan, at his peak, was considered one of the most powerful people in the world. As chairman of the Board of Governors of the Federal Reserve, he monitored inflation. It was his final recommendation that determined if interest rates would rise or fall. As a public servant his income topped out at $180,000 a year. That isn't bad but, now that he is retired and off his assets, he commands $150,000 per speaking engagement; and he signed a book deal with Penguin Press for $8 million.

What assets are you sitting on?

The Company You Keep

It is not so much our friends' help that helps us as the confident knowledge that they will help us.
—*Epicurus*

Second only to your belief in yourself, the company you keep has the greatest influence on your life and success.

After I dropped out of high school I ran into a family friend who had just bought a new Nissan 300z. When the 300z came out, it was the hottest car around. Our friend was a vice president of big box store and was probably the most successful person I knew. He not only had one 300z; he had two—one for himself and one for his wife. It was my first experience with wealth and what it could do. He asked me if I wanted to go for a ride and then threw me the keys. At 16, when you have dropped out of high school and totaled your father's favorite car, you are not feeling very confident. When someone of a higher position puts that kind of trust in you it changes you. I took that car to 120 mile per hour as quickly as it would get there. He didn't say a word.

Never before had a relative stranger put that much trust in me; so I slowed the car down and we talked about my future. He took a real interest in my desire to be self employed. After graduation, he helped me order T-shirts for my screen printing business. When I came home during Christmas break from college, he put me to work at his second home, chopping wood.

Years later my parents, wife and I took a trip to Ireland by way of New York, where we took in a Broadway show. As luck would have it, our friend sat down right in front of us. I hadn't seen him for about eight years. At the time I was at the peak of my success, before the market crashed; and I was able to pull him aside and thank him for his influence. I know if I called him today he would be there to help.

The Company You Keep

Your associations will either help or destroy you. Richard Branson relates this story in **Losing My Virginity: How I've Survived, Had Fun, and Made a Fortune Doing Business My Way**. When Branson was getting Virgin Records off the ground, he had an opportunity to sign a new band he liked. He took the band to his favorite restaurant after working out the terms of the deal. The restaurateur, whom Branson knew, brought out a platter with 10 marijuana joints after the meal. This was the 70s and, so as not to offend the owner, everyone accepted the gift. The next morning the band called Branson and told him they had decided to sign with Poly-Gram rather than Virgin. The deal had been all set, just awaiting a signature. Ten years later Branson learned from a book he was reading why the band had backed out. According to the book, the band did not sign because they thought Virgin had tried to trick them into signing by getting them stoned.

Branson calculated that his friendship with the restaurateur had cost his company $500 million.

What price do you put on the people you associate with? Because I grew up in just one house, never moving during my childhood, I was able to make long-lasting friendships. Two friends in particular galvanized my character in my youth. As I look back over the last 32 years, I have never known a day without these two friends.

As teenagers, we were heavily into cycling. We had the best gear, and it didn't come cheap. At a local cycling store I noticed the cabinet that held the pedals was unlocked and halfway cracked. Under the pressure to acquire a new set of racing pedals I wanted to use my five-finger discount card (shoplifting) and get a pair. As I reached in to grab them and put them into my jacket, one of my friends looked at me and scowled. When you have known someone for a long time, all they have to do is look at you to communicate. Knowing what he meant, I put the pedals back and told the owner about the unlocked cabinet. She praised me for my honesty and for helping her protect her store. Months later I went back to the same store and applied for a job. The owner remembered me and hired me on the spot.

If we realized the lasting effects on ourselves of the people we associate with, wouldn't we be more selective? Is there someone among your circle of friends who is bringing down your potential? Is there someone who has prevented you from achieving your goal?

Millionaire Dropouts

Milton Hershey's life was drastically changed by the company he kept. He dropped out of fourth grade because his father was dragging his family all over the country searching for the next get-rich-quick scheme—chasing the dollar instead of his passion. Hershey's father failed in over 17 business ventures. Hershey's mother had enough, and they separated. She put Hershey to work as an apprentice for a printer. He was fired by the third month. Eventually he found himself at home as a confectioner's apprentice.

By 19 he felt confident enough with his trade to open his first sweets shop, in Pennsylvania. He made a go of it; his father caught wind of what he was doing and wanted to enlist his vast experience into the business—and soon ran the mildly successful business into the ground. Father and son moved west, trying different businesses along the way. During this time Hershey filed for bankruptcy. Eventually, they ended up in Denver, where they tried mining. Hershey failed at mining and moved from Denver to Chicago to New York, then back to Lancaster, Pennsylvania.

In Lancaster, his mother and aunt said they would support another business venture, with one condition: his father could not be involved. Hershey agreed and started making caramels. In 1887, at the age of 30, he got a break. He was working at his sweets shop, when an Englishman came in and placed a large order to take caramels back to England to sell.

Hershey needed working capital to fill the order. He went from bank to bank to get a loan and was turned down because of his track record and that of his father. But Hershey didn't quit. He went to even more banks. Eventually, a banker took pity on him an gave him a personal short-term loan. He was then able to get the necessary supplies and fill the order. From that point on, he was never poor again. By the turn of the century and at the age of 43, Hershey was the largest manufacture of caramels in the U.S. That same year he sold the caramel company for $1 million, with the condition that he would not go into the caramel business.

With his newfound wealth and free time, Hershey focused on a project that he hoped would change the world: he wanted to build a town that would be a model of an ideal society. He knew a town would need an industry and he decided to build his town around the production of chocolate. In 1902 he scouted the east coast for an ideal location for his Chocolate Town. He settled in Dauphin County, Pennsylvania, a mile from where he was born. In 1903 construction began on a huge, modern chocolate factory. But after several years and hundreds of failed attempts he did not have a recipe that worked to make milk chocolate.

One day, Hershey inspected a vat filled with a silky milk solution

The Company You Keep

that blended easily with the chocolate. The worker who created the solution, John Schmalback, was not one of Hershey's college-educated chemists; he was a regular floor employee. Schmalback's breakthrough had been to dissolve a high concentration of sugar in the milk and then boil it slowly at low temperature in a vacuum. Now he had a product to manufacture in his new facility. By 1907 at the age of 50, Hershey introduced Hershey Kisses. By the end of the year, his chocolate sales reached $2 million. During World War II, Hershey supplied one billion chocolate bars to the armed forces. As a philanthropist, he formed a school for underprivileged children to get the education he never did. Upon his death in 1945, at 88, he left his entire estate to the school. By 2005, the school continued to be the largest shareholder of Hershey stock. It controls billions of dollars in assets and 76 percent of the voting shares in the company. This money continues to fund the education of more than a 1,000 students a year.

How different would the world be if Milton Hershey did not take the advice of his mother and dissociate himself from his father? Just ask the many thousands of students whose lives have been greatly affected because of his generosity. Would he have ever built the Hershey empire with his dad? What empire are you missing out on right now because of your associations?

Being successful isn't only about financial empires. The people you associate with can help you achieve all types of success in your life.

Think back to when you were a kid in elementary school, picking teams for recess games. The captains always picked the best players first. Kids are ruthless. I should know; I was always picked last. It didn't matter if you were the team captain's best friend. He was going to pick the best players first, regardless of your relationship. As adults we don't want to alienate our friends by picking them last. But would you ask advice from your fat friend on fitness? Would you listen to financial advice from a debt-laden friend. What about taking advice on faith from an agnostic? It sounds silly now when I put it into those contexts, but look back on your mind shifts and your assets. Which friends will assist you to be the best you are capable of? A while back I was given financial advice that I have lived by ever since: Never take financial advice from someone who makes less then you. Simple but true. Apply that same advice to the five F's:

- **Never take advice about faith** from someone who doesn't pray.
- **Never take advice about family and friends** from someone who doesn't value relationships.
- **Never take advice about fitness** from someone who is heavier than you.
- **Never take advice about finances** from someone who makes less than you.
- **Never take advice about the future** from someone who dwells on the past.

This may seem drastic, but look at the results your friends have before taking advice from them. Wouldn't you want to take advice from someone who has wisdom instead of knowledge? Hyrum Smith, founder of Franklin Covey Co., once said that wisdom is "knowledge rightly applied." Let us be wise in the advice we give and in hearing the advice we receive.

> I have friends in overalls whose friendship I would not swap for the favor of the kings of the world.
> —*Thomas A. Edison*

Who You Listen To

One of the greatest partnerships in TV history was Hanna–Barbera. William Hanna met Joseph Barbera at MGM animation studios. They were co-workers until MGM closed down its animation division. Taking this challenge in stride, Hanna convinced Barbera that they should collaborate and open their own animation studio. Together they developed Huckleberry Hound, Tom and Jerry, Yogi Bear, the Flintstones, Johnny Quest, the Banana Splits and Scooby Doo—some of the best-loved cartoon television shows and full-length movies of the twentieth century.

The Company You Keep

What would have happened to Barbera if he hadn't listened to Hanna's entreaties to join forces? Would Tom and Jerry have been developed by Hanna–Smith or Hanna–Jones Productions?

Be selective in whose advice you take. Once again, the company you keep will be the greatest single influence on your life and your success other than your own ambition.

Here's a true story: Two guys go for a drive. They're out in the middle of orange groves, with nobody around. Walter stops the car and starts pointing in different directions, talking about some wild plan for some crazy thing he's going to build. He tries to talk Arthur into investing in some of the surrounding property. Arthur says he'll think about it, but he never follows through.

Walter was Walt Disney. Arthur was Art Linkletter. And the orange groves became Disneyland.

Connecting the Dots

> Obstacles are those frightful things you see when you take your eyes off your goal.
> —Henry Ford

Have you ever taken the time to look back on your life and connect the dots to see why you are where you are? Doing so is a powerful way to discover where you are and what it will take to get to where you want to be. You may be completely satisfied with where you are now, but in the future you may want to aim for a new goal. If we aren't growing, we are dying.

By embracing your previous mind shifts you realize why you make the decisions you do. That makes it easier to face new, challenging decisions. This book was inspired by the advice a friend gave me to make a bulleted biography of my life. I sat down and just listed my bullets—the major things that have happened to me in my life, from dropping out of school, tearing down the walls at work, getting burned on royalties, losing a million dollars and starting from scratch more times than I can count.

When I was done with the list, I connected the dots (my mind shifts) and saw a pattern: Every major change in my life or career is inspired by a tragedy or a challenge. I throw caution to the wind, embrace the inevitable and just go for it. By connecting the dots I saw that I have always risked everything I own for each new business opportunity. Knowing that, it was easier to start this book.

When I started, my wife and I had the mortgage company and real estate business going strong; and I was working on new inventions and product designs. Personal tragedy struck three months into this project. I lost one of my best friends, my father-in-law, Gordon Langford. He always lived his life to the fullest, living without fear.

We sold all we had and put our time and money into this book as well as our professional speaking business. The mortgage business and real estate business has fallen by the wayside. Some people have cautioned me that it was too risky to start over in a new line of work. But I figure that, if you are reading this, then it was all worth it.

You can only control the future when you connect the dots of your past. Your future is easy to plan when you know why you make the decisions you do. You do this by connecting the dots of your previous mind shifts.

In the five F's, what mind shifts set you on the course you are on today? Connect the dots looking back and see in each of the five F's where you had a mind shift. You may have more in some areas than in others.

CONNECT YOUR DOTS to see why you are where you are today.

- **Faith**

    1. _____
    2. _____
    3. _____
    4. _____
    5. _____

- **Family and friends**

    1. _____
    2. _____
    3. _____
    4. _____
    5. _____

- **Fitness**

    1. _____
    2. _____
    3. _____
    4. _____
    5. _____

- **Finances**

    1. _____
    2. _____
    3. _____
    4. _____
    5. _____

- **Future**

    1. _____
    2. _____
    3. _____
    4. _____
    5. _____

Connecting the Dots

Knowing the power of understanding your mind shifts, where are you going to be in one week in each of the five F's?

- **Faith**

    1. _____
    2. _____
    3. _____
    4. _____
    5. _____

- **Family and friends**

    1. _____
    2. _____
    3. _____
    4. _____
    5. _____

- **Fitness**

    1. _____
    2. _____
    3. _____

Millionaire Dropouts

4. _____

5. _____

- **Finances**

    1. _____

    2. _____

    3. _____

    4. _____

    5. _____

- **Future**

    1. _____

    2. _____

    3. _____

    4. _____

    5. _____

Where will you be in one month?

- **Faith**

    1. _____

    2. _____

Connecting the Dots

3. _____

4. _____

5. _____

- **Family and friends**

    1. _____

    2. _____

    3. _____

    4. _____

    5. _____

- **Fitness**

    1. _____

    2. _____

    3. _____

    4. _____

    5. _____

- **Finances**

    1. _____

    2. _____

3. _____

4. _____

5. _____

- **Future**

    1. _____

    2. _____

    3. _____

    4. _____

    5. _____

Finally, where are you going to be in one year?

- **Faith**

    1. _____

    2. _____

    3. _____

    4. _____

    5. _____

- **Family and friends**

    1. _____

Connecting the Dots

    2. _____

    3. _____

    4. _____

    5. _____

- **Fitness**

    1. _____

    2. _____

    3. _____

    4. _____

    5. _____

- **Finances**

    1. _____

    2. _____

    3. _____

    4. _____

    5. _____

- **Future**

    1. _____

2. _____

3. _____

4. _____

5. _____

Regardless of what people tell you, you are in control of your life, and that means you can blame no one for your mistakes. If you are willing to accept that, then take advantage of your inner strength to live the way we were born to live.

Congratulations!
You are a
Millionaire Dropout graduate!

Biographical Sketches

On the following pages you will find brief biographical sketches of billionaire and millionaire dropouts who have gone before you. Some are historical figures and others are very much alive today. They all have lessons to teach by their examples.

Of the handful of billionaires in the world, a remarkable percentage are dropouts. That's why I've started with them, followed by a few people who were millionaires when millionaires were as rare as billionaires are today. The rest of the individuals are grouped roughly according to what they did to become millionaires.

I hope you enjoy reading about them.

Millionaire Dropouts Trivia

The richest man in the world eleven years running, Bill Gates, with a net worth of $50 billion, is a dropout.

Billionaires

Billionaires

Billionaires

Billionaires

Billionaires

Billionaires

Billionaires

Billionaires

Billionaires

David Geffen

BIRTH NAME David Geffen
BORN February 21, 1943
DROPPED OUT University of Texas at Austin

A POWERFUL NEW Hollywood mogul, David Geffen has lived an extraordinary life, his fortunes rising and falling with his career. He has remained upbeat through it all and come back better and stronger after each setback. Born in Brooklyn, New York, to Ukrainian immigrants Abraham and Batya Geffen, David learned basic business skills from his parents, who manufactured and sold bras. He was not interested in school from an early age but was fascinated by music and movies. David joined the University of Texas at Austin but dropped out to follow his dream to make a name in the entertainment industry.

Geffen's first job was as an usher at the CBS-TV studios, but he soon landed a job at the William Morris Agency, the largest and most prestigious talent agency of the time. Within a few years, he earned the reputation of being the hottest agent. He joined Ashley Famous Agency in 1968, when they offered him $1,000 per week. Geffen was responsible for bringing together Neil Young with Crosby, Stills and Nash for their Woodstock performance.

In Los Angeles, his mentor, Ahmet Ertugen from Atlantic Records suggested he start his own label. In 1971 Geffen formed Asylum Records. Some of the artists he signed became top-selling musicians of the 1970s, including newcomers like Jackson Browne and the Eagles and established musicians like Bob Dylan, Linda Ronstadt and Joni Mitchell.

In 1972, Geffen sold Asylum Records to Warner Bros. and for the next few years tried his hand at different ventures, eventually opening the nightclub Roxy. He became vice chairman of Warner Brothers Pictures. After clashing with the chairman, Ted Ashley, Geffen was sent to New York as an executive assistant to Steve Ross.

These years were a low point in his life as he was also misdiagnosed with bladder cancer.

The early 1980s were more rewarding. In 1980 Geffen formed Geffen Records and signed musicians like Donna Summer and John Lennon. Two days after the release of his album *Double Fantasy*, John Lennon was killed. The album sold millions and became a money-spinner for Geffen Records. Elton John was the third artist Geffen signed to the new label. In 1987 the company signed Guns N' Roses and later Nirvana, changing people's perception that the company only promoted "tired" artists. During the same decade, Geffen diversified, producing Broadway musicals like *Dreamgirls* and *Cats* and movies like *Personal Best, Risky Business* and *Little Shop of Horrors*. He sold Geffen Records to MCA in 1990, for an estimated $550 million, becoming the first self-made billionaire in Hollywood.

Geffen was now a bona fide Hollywood mogul and in 1994 founded DreamWorks SKG, with Steven Spielberg and Jeffery Katzenberg. The studio produced several successful and award-winning films, including *Saving Private Ryan, American Beauty* and *Shrek*.

Geffen has a magnetic personality that his former roommate Joni Mitchell immortalized in her song "Free Man in Paris." Over the years he has been linked to famous woman including Marlo Thomas and Cher. In 1992 he publicly acknowledged he was gay after being pressured by gay rights activist to come forward.

David Geffen is seen as a man who held nothing sacred in his quest to become rich. He has often forsaken relationships to reach his goals. After his incredible climb to wealth, he learned that money isn't everything, it can't buy happiness.

H. Wayne Huizenga

BIRTH NAME Harry Wayne Huizenga
BORN December 29, 1937
DROPPED OUT Calvin College

WAYNE HUIZENGA IS the cofounder of Waste Management, Inc., the largest waste management firm in the world. He is also the man who made Blockbuster Video a household name, opening a new store approximately every 17 hours in the early 1990s. Huizenga is known to some as a ruthless businessman and to others as an intuitive strategist, being able to combine practical business knowledge with diplomatic skill.

Huizenga was born in Chicago into a family of Dutch immigrants who had started the first garbage collecting company of the city. His father, Harry Huizenga, a carpenter by trade, moved the family to Florida to capitalize on the real estate boom there. Wayne learned to disregard the turmoil in his parents' relationship and performed well in school, taking part in sports and school politics. He entered Calvin College, in Michigan, in 1956, but dropped out less than two years later. He trained with the Army Reserves for six months, got married and moved back to Fort Lauderdale, joining Pompano Carting, a waste disposal company.

With real estate booming and new houses and suburbs being constructed, garbage collection was a lucrative business. Huizenga convinced Wilbur Porter, of Porter's Rubbish Service, to sell him a truck and a list of customers in 1962. Over the next seven years, he expanded his business to become one of the largest in the area.

In his drive to succeed, Huizenga developed obsessive work habits, which often led to him venting his anger and frustrations on others, allegedly including his wife, Joyce. After six years of marriage, she filed for divorce, citing extreme cruelty to her and her two sons. In 1971, Huizenga married Marti Goldsby, a secretary at his firm, Southern Sanitation Service.

Seeing the growth potential in the waste collection business, Huizenga and Dean Buntrock formed Waste Management Inc., (WMI) in 1971. They consolidated the fractured industry by buying out smaller firms. Within the next ten years WMI became the largest waste disposal company in the world. Huizenga had become a business magnate through ambition and hard work. He retired in 1983 and purchased several service companies dealing in laundry, lawn care and pest control in Florida.

Huizenga first visited a Blockbuster video store in 1987 and was so impressed he decided to buy the company. Applying his standard procedures of targeting small firms, buying them outright or driving them out of business and then increasing the fees, he hiked the fees drastically at Blockbuster. Although his aggressive tactics led to a phenomenal growth in the company, Blockbuster has faced several lawsuits regarding discrimination over the years.

Huizenga was named as one of the ten most powerful people in the entertainment industry by *Entertainment Weekly* in 1994. After merging Blockbuster with Viacom in 1994 Huizenga started AutoNation, a nationwide auto dealership that offered a fixed price, and then a hotel chain called Extended Stay America.

In an effort to improve his image, Huizenga decided to invest in sports. He started a baseball team, naming them the Florida Marlins. In the following years, he also brought the Florida Panthers to town and then purchased the Miami Dolphins, becoming a folk hero in the region.

Ambition, restlessness and driving passion have made Wayne Huizenga what he is today. He bought companies, made them profitable and sold them for millions, making success look easy.

Steve Jobs

BIRTH NAME Steven Paul Jobs
BORN February 24, 1955
DROPPED OUT Reed College

Steve Jobs, the genius responsible for popularizing the concept of personal computers, is the co-founder and CEO of Apple Computers. Widely known for his passion for innovative technology and design, Jobs also drove the development of the wildly popular iPod.

Born in Los Altos, California, to unmarried parents, he was adopted by Paul and Clara Jobs and grew up in Mountain View, California. Steve showed keen interest in building things, solving problems and attending engineering lectures at Hewlett-Packard after school, even working there in the summer. After graduation from Homestead High School in 1972, he moved to Portland, Oregon, to enroll in Reed College; but he dropped out after one semester.

Returning to California, Jobs took a position as a technician at video game manufacturer Atari. In 1976, he co-founded Apple Computer, Inc., with Steve Wozniak, famously starting the company in a garage. They manufactured their first personal computer, Apple I, and sold it for $666. They introduced the updated Apple II in 1977, and it was successful in the home segment. In 1983, they introduced a new prototype, Lisa, with the first commercial graphical user interface and mouse. Although its price tag of $10,000 doomed it to failure in the market, it did create a demand that made the launch of the Macintosh, the following year, a tremendous success. Apple's progress was held back, as the operating systems used by the company differed in each of its initial computers, and these operating systems were not compatible with IBM computers that were dominating the market.

In 1984, with the launch of the Macintosh, it became possible for workers who had no programming background to begin using personal computers at the office. The ability to point, click and drag instead of typing commands at an operating system prompt changed forever the way people perceived computers.

After a power struggle with CEO John Sculley in 1985, Jobs was stripped of his powers and he resigned from the company. He went on to found NeXT, Inc., which made some breakthroughs in advancing computer technology, but their products were too expensive to be commercially viable.

Apple Computers purchased NeXT in 1996 for $402 million, making Jobs CEO in 1997. He took the company forward by branching out into the field of personal electronics with the iPod portable music player and iTunes. Jobs also focused on the power of branding and offered innovative designs in his computers.

In 1986, Jobs purchased Pixar Animation Studios from George Lucas. Pixar hit the big time a decade later with Toy Story and after that produced several award winning films, including Finding Nemo and The Incredibles.

Jobs married Laurene Powell in 1991. They live with their three children in Silicon Valley, close to where he grew up among the apple and apricot orchards. These orchards are where he got the name of his first company, Apple. Jobs remains a true innovator and diehard perfectionist. He once said, "Innovation distinguishes between a leader and a follower." He is reputed to be a great motivator although not necessarily a team player. A visionary who followed his dreams even at the cost of losing his company, Steve Jobs revolutionized the world by making personal computers available to the common man.

Millionaire Dropouts Trivia

Asia's richest resident, Li Ka-shing, worth $18.8 billion, is a high school dropout.

Ray Kroc

BIRTH NAME Ray Kroc
BORN October 5, 1902
DIED January 14, 1984
DROPPED OUT High School

FOUNDER OF THE McDonald's Corporation, Ray Kroc revolutionized the fast food industry. *Time* quotes a Harvard Business School professor described him as "the service sector's equivalent of Henry Ford."

Kroc was born in Oak Park, Illinois, in 1902. Eager to serve in World War I, he dropped out of school in 1917, lying about his age to become a Red Cross ambulance driver; but the war ended before he could be sent to Europe. He then found a job playing the piano on the radio, as he was an accomplished player.

In 1922, Kroc started selling cups for the Tulip Cup Company. While traveling, he met Earl Prince, inventor of a new Multimixer milkshake machine. Kroc was able to judge its sales potential and got the exclusive rights to sell the Multimixer. He was soon traveling across the U.S. promoting and selling it. In San Bernardino, California, he met the McDonald brothers, who ran a restaurant and had ordered eight Multimixers from him. Kroc was impressed with the efficient way they operated and offered to set-up nationwide franchises for them.

In 1955, Kroc opened his first McDonald's, just outside Chicago, and following the Mcdonald brothers' original low cost and low service approach he offered fast food at the lowest possible prices. In 1961, Kroc bought out the McDonald brothers for $2.7 million. By 1963, McDonald's had sold three billion burgers and had opened its 500th restaurant. Kroc established his 1000th restaurant in 1968 and was soon exploring expansion in Europe, opening his first restaurant there in 1971.

Kroc's decision to target children could not have been better timed. The baby boom led to McDonald's becoming an accepted part of an American family's life, with its child-centric menu, play zones and the new icon of the company, Ronald McDonald. The clown was to become so popular that for most children he was more recognizable than the U.S. president.

Seeing trends and shifts in popular culture ahead of others, Kroc offered Americans a place "to eat, not dine," a casual and friendly restaurant, where there was no waiting and no reservations. Kroc was well known for his dedication to high standards, offering "quality, service, cleanliness and value" under efficient leadership. He created a chain of restaurants that were almost identical across the world, while still maintaining the core principles of the company. A consummate salesman, Kroc changed the way Americans eat and what they think of fast food.

Kroc was named American of the Year in 1973. After retirement, he focused on charity work and sports. He became the owner of the San Diego Padres in 1974. Kroc died of a heart attack in 1984.

Ray Kroc never stopped innovating. He tried to open an upscale version of McDonalds; he set up tavern-themed restaurants and pie shops; but these ventures were not successful. He had a strong sense of trends, strongly believed in his vision and had an indefatigable drive to succeed. Although he did not invent fast food, he presented it in a novel way, winning the hearts of an entire generation and more.

Millionaire Dropouts Trivia

Argentina's sole billionaire, Gregorio Perez, worth $1.7 billion, is a high school dropout.

John D. Rockefeller Sr.

BIRTH NAME John Davison Rockefeller
BORN July 8, 1839
DIED May 23, 1937
DROPPED OUT High School

JOHN D. ROCKEFELLER, the capitalist and renowned philanthropist who created Standard Oil, was born in Richford, New York to William A. and Eliza Davison Rockefeller. As a child, John lived in Monrovia and Owego, New York, before moving to Cleveland, Ohio, in 1853. He was a good student, excelling in math and on the debating team, both skills that helped him in life. John's father was a traveling salesman; the main influence in John's life was his mother, who taught him to work hard, save money and donate to charities.

Leaving high school in 1855, Rockefeller enrolled in Folsom Mercantile College for a six-month business course, completing it in three months and joining commission merchant firm Hewitt & Tuttle as a bookkeeper. By 1859, he started a commission business in partnership with Maurice B. Clark. The partners invested in an oil refinery, as Cleveland was gaining stature as an important refining center.

Rockefeller, along with his brother William, Henry M. Flagler and others, formed The Standard Oil Company in 1870, with $1 million in capital. In two years, the company had bought all the small refineries in Cleveland. In addition to his interests in the oil industry, Rockefeller invested in iron mines, timber plantations and factories. He also played an important part in the establishment of Chase Manhattan Bank.

The Standard Oil Company controlled approximately 90 percent of petroleum production in the U.S. by 1879 and had set up a distribution system covering nearly every town in America. Standard was aggressive. The company engaged in practices that led to its unpopularity with competitors, but customers liked their low prices. Rockefeller built a network of companies under the Standard Oil Trust, which the public eventually came to see as evil, leading to the antitrust movement. In a landmark judgment in 1911, the Supreme Court declared Standard Oil to be a monopoly and ordered it broken up into smaller companies. A total of 34 new companies were formed including those that became Chevron, Exxon, Mobil and Conoco.

In 1896, Rockefeller retired from active involvement in Standard Oil, although he remained president of the company until 1911. He then focused on philanthropy. As a boy, he gave most of his earnings to the church, and the tradition of charity and helping others was deeply ingrained in him. He contributed and ensured others' donations to found the University of Chicago. In 1901, he set up the Rockefeller Institute for Medical Research, later named The Rockefeller University, to discover causes of diseases and how to prevent them. In another effort to improve education, he formed the General Education Board (GEB) to promote education without "distinction of race, sex or creed". The Rockefeller Sanitary Commission worked between 1909 and 1915 to eradicate hookworm disease in the south. The Rockefeller Foundation was formed in 1913 to "promote the well-being of mankind throughout the world". Rockefeller also made personal donations to several universities, theological schools, Baptist missionary organizations and YMCAs and YWCAs.

Rockefeller married Laura Celestia Spelman in 1864; they had four daughters and one son, John D. Jr, who inherited most of the family fortune. John D. Rockefeller Sr. died at his home in Ormond Beach, Florida in 1937.

Rockefeller was not in the business of making money. He followed his passion for work and his instinct to stay ahead of the times; money was a byproduct. He once said, "I believe the power to make money is a gift from God. ... Having been endowed with the gift I possess, I believe it is my duty to make money and still more money, and to use the money I make for the good of my fellow man according to the dictates of my conscience."

J.R. Simplot

BIRTH NAME John Richard Simplot
BORN January 9, 1909
DROPPED OUT High School

J.R. SIMPLOT IS the founder of the J.R. Simplot Company, one of the largest privately owned companies in the world. His company is famous for inventing the procedure to produce high quality frozen french fries and is the largest supplier of french fries to McDonald's. J.R. Simplot was born in Dubuque, Iowa, in 1909 to Charles Richard and Dorothy Simplot. The family lived in the Snake River valley in Idaho and J.R. dropped out of school in the eighth grade when he left home after fighting with his father.

In 1923, Simplot decided to go into business for himself. He leased 120 acres near Declo, Idaho, to grow potatoes. Observing that the market for hogs was down, he set up a hog feeding operation with his father's help. He fed over three hundred hogs through the winter, on potatoes he grew and wild horses he caught, and sold them the following spring for a $7,000 profit. He used that money to buy horses and more land to start potato farming in earnest. In 1928, He bought a potato sorting machine and by the start of World War II had became the largest potato farmer in Idaho, shipping out 5,000 rail cars per season. Simplot noticed the shortage of fertilizers during the war and built a manufacturing plant in Pocatello, Idaho. It was this quick thinking and problem solving, combined with ambition and restless energy that led to his tremendous success.

By branching out into potato and vegetable processing, Simplot capitalized on the huge market of supplying dehydrated onions and potatoes to the military. The company also mined iron ore, had a fish farm and supplied hamburger patties. In 1946, company chemist Ray Dunlap invented a process to make frozen french fries that would not turn soggy. This innovation revolutionized the way fast food companies like McDonald's functioned. An estimated 40 percent of the company's profit comes from supplying McDonald's with frozen french fries.

As a high school dropout, Simplot relied on intuition and common sense. As the company grew, he stayed in touch with the workings of his company, making sure he knew how to do the job himself before delegating it to someone else. A strong believer in rejuvenating the American West, he also invested in several unrelated projects, making sudden decisions based more on gut feelings than business acumen.

Simplot transferred his voting stock to his children in the early 1960s and in 1973 retired as president. His eldest son, Richard, died in 1993. His second son, Donald, was not interested in education and had married five times. His daughter, Gay, was more interested in looking after the civic affairs of the company. Only his youngest son, Scott, is actively involved in the business.

By the 1980s the company had lost its innovative edge and its larger divisions were not growing, although they were profitable. J.R. decided to make another offbeat investment. in a start-up company called Micron Technology Inc., which made memory chips. Surprising everyone, the company was successful and its stock became highly sought after. Simplot earned millions from that investment. He retired from the board of J.R. Simplot Company in 1994, making way for the new generation of Simplots.

J.R.'s contributions to the potato industry have been honored in the World Potato Congress and the Idaho Potato Hall of Fame. Currently, he lives in downtown Boise with his wife, Esther.

Not only was J.R. Simplot a leader himself but he also inspired others to lead with him rather than just follow. The continuing success of his company is a testament to the fighting spirit that he instilled in his employees. His is one of the great success stories of twentieth-century America.

Steven Spielberg

BIRTH NAME Steven Allan Spielberg
BORN December 18, 1946
DROPPED OUT California State University, Long Beach

STEVEN SPIELBERG WAS born in Cincinnati, Ohio, and grew up in Haddonfield, New Jersey, and later Scottsdale, Arizona. Encouraged by his mother, Leah, Steven made his first film when he was 12; an eight-minute western titled *The Last Gun*. He was soon making longer and technically superior films, mostly based on World War II.

Spielberg enrolled in California State University at Long Beach to study English, after he was turned down twice for a film course at the University of Southern California. He got a job with Universal Studios, where he made a short film called *Amblin*; this won an award at the Atlanta Film Festival and got him a seven-year contract with the studio. During this time, Spielberg directed episodes of several TV shows, including *Marcus Welby MD*, *The Name of the Game* and *Colombo*. His first TV movie, *Duel*, got him noticed and led to more movies, such as *Something Evil* and *Sugarland Express*, which was his own project and won him an award for best screenplay at the Cannes Film Festival.

The movie *Jaws*, an adaptation of Peter Benchley's book, took Spielberg to the big leagues. It was an astounding success and Spielberg became Hollywood's golden boy. *Close Encounters of the Third Kind*, a sci-fi thriller, was his next film. His one and only failure was *1941*, a comedy set in wartime Pearl Harbor. From then on, Spielberg made one blockbuster after another, always experimenting and pushing audiences a little bit further each time. Some of his most successful movies include *Raiders of the Lost Ark*, *ET: The Extra Terrestrial*, *The Twilight Zone*, *Indiana Jones and the Temple of Doom*, *Poltergeist*, and *Gremlins*. Other well-received movies include *Empire of the Sun, Always, Hook* and *The Color Purple. Jurassic Park* featured awe-inspiring special effects and became, with its sequel, *The Lost World,* among the highest-grossing movies of all time.

The starkly portrayed emotional drama, *Schindler's List,* a story of a Nazi who risked his life to save Jews from extermination camps, was Spielberg's ten-year-long dream and one of his finest movies. He won Oscars for best picture and best director for it. In 1994, Spielberg set up Dreamworks, a multimedia production company, with fellow dropout David Geffen and Jeffrey Katzenberg.

Saving Private Ryan, a superbly crafted, large-scale World War II movie, showed the Normandy landing in great detail. Spielberg took over *AI: Artificial Intelligence* after the death of Stanley Kubrick and created the movie through a child's eyes. In the detective genre, Spielberg made *Minority Report* and *Catch Me If You Can.*

In 2002, Spielberg finally received a degree from California State University Long Beach, the same school he had dropped out of in 1969.

The aloofness of Spielberg's father had a major impact on his life and his movies; he often depicts characters with reluctant or absent fathers. Although Spielberg has been the favorite of audiences, critics have often remarked on the lack of emotional depth in his films and on their focus on action.

Steven Spielberg has become like the legendary King Midas, turning everything he touches to gold. He has been successful in a wide range of genres, reaching out to the hearts of millions with his breathtaking special effects. Spielberg is one of the most powerful men in the history of film and Hollywood's most successful director. He blends a childlike sense of wonder with expertly crafted techniques and special effects to awe, entertain and frighten audiences.

Millionaire Dropouts Trivia

There are 67 billionaires who are dropouts and numerous millionaires.

Millionaires

Millionaires

Millionaires

Millionaires

Millionaires

Millionaires

Millionaires

Millionaires

Millionaires

John Jacob Astor

BIRTH NAME Johann Jakob Astor
BORN July 17, 1763
DIED March 29, 1848
DROPPED OUT High School

JOHN JACOB ASTOR became one of America's wealthiest men in the nineteenth century. He made a fortune in fur trading and real estate, and his name is synonymous with financial success.

Astor was born in Walldorf, Germany. At 16 he left home and his father's butcher shop to go to London, where his brother George manufactured musical instruments. In London, John helped his brother with sales as he learned English. He later traveled to New York in 1784, at the end of the Revolutionary War, to explore new markets for musical instruments. There he worked in a butcher's shop and also as a baker for a while, before he was introduced to the fur trade, starting his own shop later in the decade.

Astor started exploring New York for fur trade and for business connections and also met fur traders from Montreal, Canada. In the late 1780s, he set up a fur goods shop in New York and became a leading businessman in the trade. He soon started shipping fur to London and importing musical instruments on the returning ships. He also greatly benefited by the Jay Treaty between Great Britain and the new United States, which opened markets in Canada and the Great Lakes region.

When he married Sarah Todd, who was more than willing to help him, his business grew even larger. He started shipping fur, tea and sandalwood to China, as American traders did not need permission to trade in ports monopolized by the East India Company.

In 1808, Astor established the American Fur Company and its subsidiaries, the Pacific Fur Company and the Southwest Fur Company.

Astor's trade suffered when, during the War of 1812, the British captured his trading posts. But five years later the U.S. Congress barred foreign traders from U.S. territories, and his business bounced back. It once again thrived in the area around the Great Lakes. The Astor House on Mackinac Island became the headquarters for the American Fur Company. When the demand for fur declined because of changing fashions, Astor, being a shrewd investor, turned to real estate and made a fortune in that business, too.

Astor retired from business in 1834 to devote his time to philanthropy. He founded the Astor Library in New York and built a poorhouse in Walldorf, where he was born. He also set up the first hotel that belonged to the Astor family. He took active part in the presidential campaign of Henry Clay and became close friends with well-known ornithologist John James Audubon and the writer Edgar Allan Poe.

At the time of his death in 1848, he left an estate estimated to be worth $20 million. John Jacob Astor's driving ambition and shrewd business acumen made him America's first multimillionaire.

Millionaire Dropouts Trivia

Spain's richest resident, Amancio Ortega, worth $14.8 billion, is a high school dropout.

Andrew Carnegie

BIRTH NAME Andrew Carnegie
BORN November 25, 1835
DIED August 11, 1919
DROPPED OUT Elementary School

BORN IN DUNFERMLINE, Scotland, into a weaver's family, Andrew Carnegie had a difficult childhood. The industrial revolution saw steam-powered looms force hand weavers out of jobs. Andrew's mother had to work to support the family; she opened a grocery shop and earned some extra money mending shoes. Andrew experienced what it meant to be poor. Watching his father beg for work, he decided early in life that making money would be his goal. His mother persuaded her husband that it would be better for the family to move to America to join other relatives already there. Borrowing £20, the family left for Pittsburgh in 1848.

William, Andrew's father, got a job in a cotton factory and Andrew himself started working as a bobbin boy in the same building. He was 13 and he earned $1.20 per week.

The Carnegie family valued education. Andrew took advantage of the offer of a local gentleman who invited working boys to borrow from his personal library. Carnegie took a new job, at $2.50 a week, as a messenger in a telegraph office, where he applied his ingenuity to further his education, by arranging to deliver messages to theatres and then staying to watch Shakespearean plays. He also attended to his job, becoming one of the few people who could accurately and quickly transcribe incoming telegraphy by ear. Thomas A. Scott, a superintendent at the Pennsylvania Railroad, noticed him and made Carnegie his private secretary and personal telegrapher, paying him $4 a week. Carnegie partnered with the inventor of the sleeping car, reaping huge profits from the sale of the cars to the railroad at the same time he rose in the railroad for speeding up rail service by introducing the sleeping cars. By the time the Civil War ended in 1865, Carnegie was superintendent of the western division of the railroad.

During the Civil War, Carnegie's old mentor, Scott, was the Assistant Secretary of War and brought Carnegie with him for a stint in Washington. Carnegie, a shrewd investor, put $40,000 into a Pennsylvania farm in 1864 and made over $1 million in dividends the following year, on the oil shipped from the farm.

With the end of the Civil War, the iron industry opened up and, sensing that it had great potential, Carnegie resigned from Pennsylvania Railroad. He set up a steel plant in Pittsburgh and put all his money into the business, starting mass production of steel rails for railroad lines. Carnegie Steel became the largest manufacturer of pig iron and steel-rails. When he purchased Homestead Steel Works in 1892, the Carnegie Steel Company was formed. The company grew. In 1901, Carnegie sold his holdings to J.P. Morgan for $480 million.

Carnegie firmly believed that the rich have a moral obligation to give away their fortunes. He wrote a book called *The Gospel of Wealth*, in which he said that all personal wealth beyond that required to fulfill the needs of one's family should be regarded as a trust fund to be used for the benefit of the community.

Having educated himself by reading books in libraries, Carnegie established over 1,600 libraries in the U.S. alone and many in other countries from Scotland to Fiji. In 1901, he donated $2 million to start the Carnegie Institute of Technology (now Carnegie Mellon University) in Pittsburgh. In 1902, he gave another $2 million to fund the Carnegie Institution in Washington. DC, and the same amount in 1901 to assist Scottish universities.

When he died in 1919, Carnegie had given away $350 million in his lifetime. In his will he left another $30 million to foundations, trusts and charities.

Charles Emory Culpeper

BIRTH NAME Charles Emory Culpepper
BORN May 11, 1874
DIED 2February 2, 1940
DROPPED OUT High School

CHARLES CULPEPER (he dropped the extra *p* from his name) was a man of extraordinary vision. He pioneered the bottling and marketing of Coca-Cola. He has left behind a legacy that supports charitable causes in education and medical research.

Charles Emory Culpepper was born in Rome, Georgia. He was one of nine children and grew up on a family farm near Rome. Charles dropped out of high school, but he was always resourceful and hard working. He worked as a clerk in a store and later became a salesman. He did various odd jobs and in 1899, he started selling Coca-Cola syrup to soda fountains in Philadelphia. In 1904, he started working full time as a salesman for the Coca-Cola Bottling Works of Newark and New York.

Thirteen years later, in 1917, Charles Culpeper bought the Newark and New York bottlers for $160,000, using borrowed funds. The two companies were later combined to form the Coca-Cola Bottling Company of New York. He took the company to new heights and, when he died in 1940, his stock in the company amounted to a major fortune.

Although he lived in Norwalk, Connecticut, from 1913 on, he always wanted to give back something to his home state of Georgia. He was a humanitarian and wanted to work for the betterment of mankind. He died February 2, 1940 and was buried at the West Union Baptist Church Cemetery, Curryville, Georgia. He had no children and left a will that said the fortune he left behind should be used to form a charitable foundation.

The Charles E. Culpeper Foundation was formed in 1940 with his personal fortune and it has contributed to various charitable causes.

At the end of 1998, the foundation had assets worth over $207 million. The same year, the foundation also granted aid close to $8.7 million for health, education, art and cultural development.

The Charles E. Culpeper Foundation of Connecticut and the Rockefeller Brothers Fund of New York merged 1 July 1999 to form the Rockefeller Brothers Fund Inc., with its investment assets at that time valued at $650 million. The Charles E. Culpeper Scholarships in Medical Science and the Charles E. Culpeper Biomedical Pilot Initiative, the two programs established under the Culpeper name, continue under the new name. Programs in health, education, arts and culture that formed a part of Culpeper's vision for the wellbeing of mankind are also being carried out under the new name.

Culpeper's life was an extraordinary one. One man's vision and exemplary zeal led to the formation of a foundation that has helped in funding research and aid in the field of medicine and education, leading to major breakthroughs in medical research. Although Culpeper did not finish his schooling, he valued education and research and contributed immensely to both fields, making the world a better place to live.

Millionaire Dropouts Trivia

**Three of the ten richest people in the world are dropouts:
number 1, Bill Gates, worth $50 billion;
number 6, Paul Allen, worth $22 billion;
number 10, Li Ka-shing, worth $18.8 billion.**

Del Webb

BIRTH NAME Delbert Eugene Webb
BORN May 17, 1899
DIED July 4, 1974
DROPPED OUT High School

DEL WEBB WAS born in Fresno, California, to wealthy pioneers Ernest and Henrietta Webb. When his father went bankrupt in 1914, Del left high school after his freshman year to help support his family, working as a carpenter's apprentice. He was interested in baseball, an interest he picked up from his father, and played semi-pro ball while working as a carpenter through the 1920s.

Webb got typhoid fever in 1927 and moved to Phoenix to recuperate. He decided to focus all his energies on construction and set up a small firm in 1928. He built a solid and reliable business using tactics that had helped him in baseball—making bold decisions, relying on teamwork and producing a steady performance even under pressure. Soon, his company became known for its ability to develop large-scale, high-quality projects, winning contracts for Madison Square Garden and the Los Angeles County Museum of Art.

During World War II, the company demonstrated to the military its ability to construct entire communities on barren land. This experience helped the company take part in the postwar boom in construction.

Webb's innovative approach to problem solving during the war led him to meet a number of influential people like Howard Hughes, with whom he shared common interests in golf and flying, and for whom he did over $1 billion worth of business. Webb returned to his first love, baseball, to buy the New York Yankees with Al Tipping in 1945. In the twenty years they owned the team, the Yankees won the World Series ten times.

Webb's company built Bugsy Siegel's Flamingo Hotel in Las Vegas in 1946, starting the gambling boom there. Webb capitalized on the rush and soon became the largest gaming operator and private employer in Nevada. The Sahara was Webb's first hotel in Las Vegas. Soon his friend Howard Hughes purchased property, improving the image of the city as a reputable place. Webb was a skilled observer of social psychology and understood and targeted the elite subculture.

In 1960, the Del Webb Corporation opened Sun City in Phoenix; the retirement community became a phenomenal success. The company decided to focus on developing active adult communities and divest from the gaming and commercial interests in 1987. Webb concentrated on building larger homes, offering more recreational and club facilities, leading the way for providing a luxurious environment. The company built thirteen Sun Cities with over 80,000 homes, and its annual revenues grew to $2 billion when it merged with Pulte Homes in 2001, becoming the largest home construction company in the country.

Webb married his childhood sweetheart Hazel. They were divorced in 1952, and in 1961 he married Toni Ince. Webb died of lung cancer in 1974. As neither marriage produced any children, most of Webb's fortune went to the Del E. Webb Foundation, funding medical projects in Arizona, California and Nevada.

Del Webb, real estate developer and former owner of the New York Yankees was a self-made man. Following his twin passions of baseball and carpentry, he forged a company from nothing just as he built communities in the Arizona desert. He relied on his creative working style, attention to detail and positive attitude to create the largest construction company in the U.S. He was a man known for his integrity, values and a strong dedication to his commitments. He was always ahead of the curve, recognizing and paving the way for independent homes for adults, capitalizing on the postwar construction boom and using innovative marketing and problem solving techniques.

Millionaire Dropouts Trivia

The world's wealthiest high school dropout is Li Ka-shing.

Founders

Founders

Founders

Founders

Founders

Founders

Founders

Founders

Founders

Wally Amos

BIRTH NAME Wallace Amos Jr.
BORN July 1, 1936
DROPPED OUT Food Trade Vocational High School

WALLY AMOS IS the inventor of Famous Amos chocolate chip cookies and founder of the company that bears the same name. He is credited with being the father of the gourmet chocolate chip cookie industry. Known as an entrepreneur, orator, philosopher and author, Amos has used his success and fame to support literacy programs and other causes.

Wally Amos was born in 1936 in Tallahassee, Florida, and lived there with his parents till the age of 12. He then moved to New York City to live with his Aunt Della. With his interest in cooking, Amos decided to enter the Food Trades Vocational High School. When he was a senior, he dropped out to join the U.S. Air Force, where he completed his GED. This changed his life and made it possible for him to train at a secretarial school in New York after he was honorably discharged from the service.

On completion of his secretarial training, he started working in a clerical position at the William Morris Agency and became the agency's first African-American talent agent, representing musical acts like Simon and Garfunkel, Diana Ross and the Supremes.

Amos was innovative in his approach. He brought clients to the Agency by sending them chocolate chip cookies with invitations to visit him. After a few years, he decided to focus on what had till then been a weekend hobby, chocolate chip cookies. He began to sell cookies based on his Aunt Della's recipe. The first Famous Amos store opened in 1975 in Los Angeles.

Amos hosted a series of programs on PBS for adult basic learners. In 1977, he became an ardent advocate for literacy in America, and in 1979, he became the national spokesman for Literacy Volunteers of America. He also became a board member of the National Center for Family Literacy and Communities in schools.

After being hired by an influential firm as a professional speaker, Amos became known for his dynamic style and an inspiring and positive attitude. He extolled the principles that made him successful. By being humble and sharing his setbacks and unfulfilled dreams, he enabled his audiences to identify with him.

Amos has received several honors and awards. He gave the shirt off his back and his trademark battered Panama hat to be displayed at the Smithsonian Institution's Business Americana Collection. Johnson & Wales University awarded him an honorary doctorate in education. He was also inducted into the Babson College Academy of Distinguished Entrepreneurs. Other awards he has received are the Horatio Alger Award; The President's Award for Entrepreneurial Excellence and The National Literacy Honors Award.

In 1983, he wrote his autobiography, *The Famous Amos Story: The Face that Launched a Thousand Chips*. He also wrote *The Power in You: Ten Secret Ingredients to Inner Strength*; and *Man with No Name: Turn Lemons into Lemonade*, where he shares his experiences of losing everything he had, including his name, and overcoming adversities by turning them into opportunities. His last book, published in 1996, was *Watermelon Magic: Seeds of Wisdom, Slices of Life*, in which he uses a watermelon as a metaphor for life and shared his philosophy and insights.

Wally Amos lives in Maui, Hawaii, and is actively involved in public speaking, sharing his dreams and philosophy of life. He focused on his drive to succeed by trusting in his invincible spirit and positive approach to life. He is a firm believer in practicing what he preaches and knew all aspects of his business closely. Even though his is a household name, he remains grounded in reality and still maintains his trademark positive spirit.

William E. Boeing

BIRTH NAME William Edward Boeing
BORN October 1, 1881
DIED September 28, 1956
DROPPED OUT Yale University

WILLIAM BOEING, THE founder of the Boeing Airplane Co., was a pioneer in the American aviation industry. His passion for flying took the aviation industry in America to new heights.

Boeing was born in Detroit. He entered the Sheffield Scientific School at Yale University but dropped out two years later, in 1903, the year the Wright brothers flew at Kitty Hawk. Boeing moved to Washington, where he built a fortune trading timber lands, settling in Seattle in 1908. He attended a public air show in California, where he became fascinated with flying and the field of aviation. In 1914, he flew for the first time, but by then he knew he wanted to build his own plane. He was confident that he could come out with a better plane than the ones that were being used at the time.

Boeing worked with his friend George Conrad Westervelt, an engineer, to design the B&W, a twin-float seaplane. He started his own company, Pacific Aero Products Co., in 1916, changing the name to the Boeing Airplane Co. a year later. The company started manufacturing airplanes in a seaplane hanger in Seattle.

In 1917, Boeing had parts of a plane shipped off to Florida to be reassembled and displayed for Navy officials to test. Boeing anticipated that the U.S. Navy would need such planes for use in World War I. His hunch proved to be right and the Navy ordered 50 planes. After the war, however, the demand for planes declined and Boeing managed to keep his company going by diversifying into building furniture and boats.

The company came out with the B-1, a biplane that created history on March 3, 1919, when Boeing and pilot Eddie Hubbard flew

Founder, William Boeing

the plane from Seattle to Vancouver. It was the first international airmail route. This service continued till the mid 1920s. Later, the company began building fighters. It started manufacturing engines and propellers as well. In 1934, Boeing received the Daniel Guggenheim Medal for successful pioneering and achievement in aircraft design and manufacturing.

In 1934, the U.S. government passed new federal laws that did not allow airmail carriers and aircraft manufacturers to be part of the same company. As orders were cancelled, William Boeing was forced to split his company into different companies. He later sold his stock in the company.

Boeing's interest in the aviation industry continued and he offered his services as a consultant to his former company during World War II. During the war the company produced the B-17, the B-29 and the Kaydet trainer. The B-17 Flying Fortress and the B-29 Super Fortress became the symbols of America's military pride. It was a Boeing B-29 Super Fortress that carried the first atomic bomb that was dropped on Japan. By the 1950s, with his health failing, William Boeing dissociated himself from the company's activities. By the time he died in 1956, the company he had founded had entered the jet age.

William Boeing set his dreams up in the sky. With his great vision, hard work and innovative ideas, his legacy in the American aviation industry is assured.

Walt Disney

BIRTH NAME Walter Elias Disney
BORN December 5, 1901
DIED December 15, 1966
DROPPED OUT High School

WALT DISNEY, THE creator of Mickey Mouse, was a pioneer, an innovator and an artist whose Hollywood career lasted 43 years. David Low, the late British political cartoonist once called him "the most significant figure in graphic arts since Leonardo DaVinci."

Walt Disney was born in Chicago, Illinois. His family moved to Marceline, Missouri, soon after Walt's birth and that was where he grew up. Interested in drawing from an early age, he drew small sketches to sell to his neighbors. His father, Elias Disney, was a strict disciplinarian. His mother, Flora Call Disney, and his brother Roy, however, encouraged him in his early years; and Walt grew up appreciating nature and wildlife. He went to McKinley High School in Chicago, where he studied both photography and drawing. He also attended the Academy of Fine Arts at night. The family later moved to Kansas City.

In 1918, Disney tried to enlist for military service but was rejected because he was only 16. So he joined the Red Cross and served in France, driving an ambulance and chauffeuring Red Cross officials. After his return from France, he started making short animated films. He ran out of money at around this time and, armed with a few drawing materials, $40 in his pocket and a copy of his film *Alice Comedies*, he left Kansas City for Hollywood. His brother Roy was already in California. Together they pooled their resources, borrowed $500 and started their production operations. After introducing Mickey Mouse in a couple of silent cartoons, Disney showed a synchronized sound version of *Steamboat Willie* at the Colony Theatre in New York on November 18, 1928, to great acclaim.

In 1932, *Flowers and Trees* won him his first Academy Award. In 1937, he made *The Old Mill,* using the multiplane camera technique for the first time. His first full-length animated musical feature *Snow White and the Seven Dwarfs* premiered at the Carthay Circle Theatre in Los Angeles. Produced at a cost of $1.5 million at the time of the Great Depression, it is considered a remarkable feat in the motion picture industry. Tragedy struck when, after the film's success, Walt moved his parents to a home close to his studio and his mother died of asphyxiation caused by a faulty furnace.

Disney went on to create animated classics such as *Pinocchio, Fantasia, Dumbo* and *Bambi*. His Burbank studio, built in 1940, had more than 1,000 artists, animators and technicians. Disney retained his interest in wildlife footage, too. Through his award winning series *True-Life Adventures,* he highlighted the importance of conserving nature.

Disneyland, opened in 1955, and was the original giant theme park. It borrowed ideas from some older-style amusement parks and smaller theme parks, but the size and originality made it a new phenomenon in the world. Disney's fanatical attention to production values and to cleanliness made the park a wholesome place for family vacations.

In thinking about the world, Disney found that the greatest challenge was to find solutions to problems faced by urban dwellers. With the idea of building a community that would become a prototype for the future, he built EPCOT Center (Experimental Prototype Community of Tomorrow), which opened on October 1, 1982, in Orlando, Florida. It is the heart of Walt Disney World Resort. The Disney-MGM Studios Theme Park opened on May 1, 1989. Walt Disney also established the California Institute of the Arts.

Winner of 48 Academy Awards, 7 Emmys and over 950 honors and citations, Walt Disney was a man whose contribution to the motion picture industry and the art of animation remains unsurpassed.

Amadeo Giannini

BIRTH NAME Amadeo Peter Giannini
BORN May 6, 1870
DIED June 3, 1949
DROPPED OUT High School

AMADEO GIANNINI FOUNDED Bank of America and is a pioneer of modern banking practices. He was the first man to come up with the unique concept of offering bank loans to poor immigrants. His sound business skills, liberal policies and innovative approach helped Bank of America become the largest banking network in America.

Amadeo Peter Giannini was born in San Jose, California, to Italian immigrant parents. When he was a small boy he saw his father killed by a man over a dollar. His widowed mother married Lorenzo Scatena, who was in the produce business. Amadeo dropped out of school to help his stepfather in his business. He worked hard and his stepfather was so impressed with him that he made Giannini a partner in the business when he was only 19 years old. In 1904, at the age of 31, he retired from the business. Being a fair-minded and honest man, Amadeo sold half the business to his employees. He had enough money and could have retired, but Giannini was a man of great vision.

He approached a few investors and, combining their money with his own, he started the Bank of Italy in 1904. In those days, loans were reserved for the rich and the creditworthy. Giannini came up with the revolutionary idea of offering loans to hardworking immigrants who were in need of money. Although home mortgages and auto loans are a common feature in any bank today, Giannini was the first person to offer such services in those days. He explained his ideas and convinced the immigrants to take loans, as they did not know much about banking. He built his business from scratch.

Founder, Amadeo Giannini

The Bank of Italy opened its doors October 17, 1904, with deposits of $8,780 on the first day.

After the 1906 San Francisco earthquake, most other banks closed; but Giannini rushed to his bank, gathered all the money, securities and gold and rushed out. He managed bank transactions on the street by placing a plank across two barrels and using it as a counter. He granted loans to people to rebuild their lives and helped reconstruct the city after the earthquake.

As his customers had to travel long distances to reach the bank, he started a branch in San Jose in 1909. He later opened several branches across the state and a few branches in other major cities across America. Thus began the first statewide banking system in the U.S. He started a holding company called Transamerica Corp. in 1928 and bought banks throughout New York, Washington, Arizona, Oregon and Nevada. He consolidated all the banks under one name—Bank of America. By 1945, despite the Great Depression, the Bank of America had grown to be the largest bank in the U.S. and the largest privately owned bank in the world.

Giannini's liberal lending policy also encouraged the agriculture sector and the motion picture industry to borrow. A generous man, he started the Bank of America–Giannini Foundation for Medical Research and Educational Scholarships. He also started the Giannini Foundation of Agricultural Economics at the University of California.

Giannini died in 1949, at the age of 79. He could have retired at 31, but his innovative ideas and great vision gave the world its largest banking network, helping ordinary, middle class and working class people build their lives and their dreams, too.

Soichiro Honda

BIRTH NAME Soichiro Honda
BORN November 17, 1906
DIED August 5, 1991
DROPPED OUT High School

Soichiro Honda is the man behind the success of the Honda Motor Company. Passionate about bikes and racing from a young age, he was instrumental in building a company that produces the largest number of motorcycles today.

Honda was born in the town of Komyo (now Tenryu) in Japan. His father was a blacksmith who also repaired bicycles. When he was young, Soichiro used to help his father in the garage.

Honda went to Tokyo in search of a job when he was 15 years old. He worked in a garage as an apprentice and later as a mechanic in an auto repair company for a few years before returning to his hometown to start his own mechanic business in 1928, at the age of 22.

Honda loved racing and took part in many racing competitions. He built his own race car using an old aircraft engine and assorted parts. In 1936, he broke several bones in a crash and stopped racing at his wife's urging.

In 1937, Honda started his own company, the Tokai Seiki Heavy Industry, to manufacture piston rings. Feeling that he had to learn a lot about casting, he went to a technical high school and applied the theories he learned there to his own factory. He did not take the exams at the end of the year though, for he did not believe in exams and certificates. Aircraft propellers mass-produced at the factory were of great help to Japanese troops during World War II. In 1948, he sold the company to Toyota for ¥450,000.

Honda started the Honda Technical Laboratory in Hamamatsu after the war. The company became known for its auxiliary bicycle engines. On September 24, 1948, the Honda Motor Company was formally established with an investment of ¥1 million. It started manufacturing engines and soon came out with the powerful Type E motorcycles, with an innovative valve design. The company expanded its operations and, in 1958, came out with the C 100 Super Cub, which became a bestseller worldwide. With the slogan "You meet the nicest people on a Honda," Honda motorcycles entered the American market in 1959.

Honda was still enthusiastic about motor racing and, in 1959, the company took part in the Isle of Man Tourist Trophy, winning the manufacturer's prize. Two years later, at the same motorcycle racing competition, Honda rode away with prizes in both the 125 cc and 250 cc categories. Honda became a household name and its exports skyrocketed. In 1965, the company entered the Formula 1 racing series. It won the Mexican Grand Prix and, a year later, won several races in the Formula 2 series.

Honda was the President of the Honda Motor Company till he retired in 1973, at the age of 67. He stayed on as its director and was appointed its supreme adviser in 1983.

Honda received the Order of the Sacred Treasure, First Class, the highest honor bestowed by Japan's emperor. He also received the American auto industry's highest award when he was admitted to the Automobile Hall of Fame in 1989. He was awarded the Automobile Manufacturer Association's highest honor, the Dud Perkins Award in 1971.

Soichiro Honda died in 1991. His passion for bikes, his innovative ideas and willingness to take risks made the Honda Motor Company one of the most respected motorcycle and automobile manufacturers in the world.

Marcus Loew

BIRTH NAME Marcus Loew
BORN May 7, 1870
DIED September 5, 1927
DROPPED OUT Elementary School

FOUNDER OF LOEWS Theatres and the famous Metro-Goldwyn-Mayer (MGM) studios, Marcus Loew was a key-figure behind the success of the American motion picture industry.

Marcus Loew was born in New York City into a family of Austrian immigrants. His mother was Ida Sichel. His father, Herman Loew, worked as a waiter. When Marcus was nine, he left school to help support his large family. He started as a newspaper boy and later took up various odd jobs, learning business skills along the way. He worked in a map-making plant, a garment shop and later in a fur factory. Marcus always dreamed of owning property and becoming a landlord.

In 1904, with the money he had saved doing various small jobs, Loew and Adolph Zukor, another immigrant as well as a fellow dropout, opened a nickelodeon in a rented store. They made enough money that Loew was able to start buying movie houses.

In 1912, Loew started Loew's Theatrical Enterprise. He bought the Metro Pictures Corporation in the early 1920s. Soon he purchased the Goldwyn Picture Corporation, which had run into financial problems. With Louis B. Mayer and Samuel Goldwyn, he formed the Metro-Goldwyn-Mayer (MGM) studio. By 1924, he had 100 theatres and by 1927, he had 144. These were deluxe, modern theatre houses that offered the best entertainment to movie and theatre enthusiasts.

In 1927, before he could see the 24 new movie houses that he had started to build, he died at the age of 57. MGM and Loew's Theatrical Enterprise, however, went on to play a major role in the American movie industry.

Founder, Marcus Loew

In 1954, when the Department of Justice ruled that theatre chains must divest themselves of studios, Loew's Theatrical Enterprise and MGM became separate entities. MGM studios went on to become the largest Hollywood film production studio, responsible for bringing out classics such as *Gone with the Wind* and *The Wizard of Oz*.

Loews Theatres merged with Cineplex Odeon Corporation in 1998 to form Loews Cineplex Entertainment, which operates in major cities across the U.S., Canada and Europe.

Driven by ambition and his love for theatre, Marcus Loew became a successful businessman, responsible for America's largest theatre chain and its biggest studio.

Millionaire Dropouts Trivia

Some of history's greatest companies were founded by dropouts, including Kodak, Polaroid, Famous Amos, Disney, Ford, Learjet, Bank of America, Motown Records, Whole Foods, Domino's, Apple Computer, Netscape, Microsoft, Polo, Jet Blue, Dunkin' Donuts, NBC, KFC, Wendy's, McDonald's, Holiday Inn and Rolling Stone Magazine.

Joseph Pulitzer

BIRTH NAME Joseph Pulitzer
BORN April 10, 1847
DIED October 29, 1911
DROPPED OUT High School

BORN IN MAKÓ, Hungary, Joseph Pulitzer was the eldest son of a grain merchant who died when Joseph was 11. His mother later married a businessman, and Joseph was educated in private schools in Budapest. At 17, he left Hungary and reached the U.S. without a penny in his pocket. Pulitzer was anxious to serve in the military, but both the Austrian Army and the French Foreign Legion had rejected him because of his frail health. He was able to serve in the Union army during the American Civil War. Pulitzer was fluent in Hungarian, German and French, but his English was not perfect. After the war, he settled in St. Louis, first working as a waiter before taking a reporting job with a German-language newspaper, the *Westliche Post*.

Pulitzer had good reporting skills. He succeeded in his work and soon bought the *Post* for $3,000, followed by the *St. Louis Dispatch* for $2,700 dollars, merging the two papers to form the *St. Louis Post-Dispatch*. He took an active part in politics and was elected to the Missouri Legislature. In 1877, he married Kate Davis.

In 1883, Pulitzer bought the New York *World* from Jay Gould. It had been losing $40,000 a year. Pulitzer increased circulation dramatically, with human-interest stories and a crusade against business monopolies. The *World* became the largest newspaper in the U.S., with a circulation of over 600,000.

Pulitzer was elected to Congress from New York in 1885, but he resigned after a few months, deciding he preferred his career in journalism. Pulitzer's paper was one of the pioneers of investigative journalism. It also published the first color comic, "The Yellow Kid."

Founder, Joseph Pulitzer

After 1890, partial blindness and failing health prevented him from taking active part in editorial duties but he continued to have financial control over the paper. The *World* got into a major circulation battle with its rival, William Randolph Hearst's Sun, famous for yellow journalism.

Pulitzer died aboard his yatch in 1911. In his will, he left $2 million to create the Graduate School of Journalism at Columbia University, which had been a long cherished dream of his. His will also established the Pulitzer Prize, to recognize excellence in the fields of journalism, music, drama and literature.

Joseph Pulitzer transformed journalism forever, with his investigative reporting, sensational stories and crusades against corruption.

Millionaire Dropouts Trivia

Titanic, the highest grossing movie of all time, was directed by a dropout (James Cameron); and the two lead actors were dropouts (Leonardo Di Caprio and Kate Winslet).

Sir Frederick Henry Royce

BIRTH NAME Frederick Henry Royce
BORN March 27, 1863
DIED April 22, 1933
DROPPED OUT Elementary School

Frederick Henry Royce was a pioneer in the motorcar industry; he created the luxurious Rolls-Royce automobile. Royce went to great lengths in his drive for perfection. His high ideals and attention to detail are followed to this day by his "boys."

Henry Royce was born in 1863 in Alwalton, England; he was nine when his father died. He dropped out of school to help support his family by delivering newspapers and telegrams. Being interested in engineering and electricity, he worked at the Great Northern Locomotive Works and then at the Electric Light and Power Company in London, becoming, at 19, the company's chief engineer at Liverpool.

Using his modest savings of £20 pounds, together with £50 invested by Ernest Claremont, he founded F.H. Royce & Company. The company manufactured simple products like electric doorbell kits, which became a big success and gave them the freedom to focus on manufacturing dynamos, electric motors and cranes. Royce's dedication to quality products was rigorous right from the start, and the company was very successful. Royce renamed the company Royce Limited in 1899 and increased his share in the company.

Soon Royce shifted his focus to making motorcars. He bought a few cars to study their engineering and decided to build two-cylinder, 10 hp cars in 1903. One of the shareholders in his company, Henry Edmunds, introduced Royce to Charles Rolls, who was looking for a replacement for the Panhard automobile. Rolls was impressed with Royce's cars and they agreed to make cars together and sell them un-

Founder, Henry Royce

der the Rolls-Royce name, with Royce focusing on the engineering and Rolls selling the cars.

By 1906, Royce had developed a 50 hp car, called the Silver Ghost, which established the company's reputation as manufacturers of the best car in the world. The Silver Ghost was the favorite car of royalty, nobility, maharajahs and heads of state. Other legendary cars produced by Rolls-Royce included the Phantom and the Wraith.

Rolls convinced Royce to become a consultant to the army for the manufacture of a swiveling propeller for the airship Gamma. When Rolls died in an airplane accident in 1911, Royce recognized the need for reliable engines for airplanes. His first aeronautical engine, Eagle, built using technology from the Silver Ghost was being used in World War I by 1916. His other aero engines, Hawk and Falcon, quickly followed.

Royce launched a second generation of engines for airplanes, the Kestral and the Buzzard, by the late 1920s and constantly worked on the engines to increase horsepower. The Merlin was developed for the Royal Air Force Hurricane and Spitfire fighter planes. His famous R engine won the Schneider Trophy for England in 1929.

Royce was awarded the Order of the British Empire after World War I and made a baronet for his contribution to British aviation in 1930. He remained actively involved in his company's engine designs till his death in 1933 at the age of 70.

Henry Royce began with no technical knowledge. But with his dedication, discipline, attitude and perfectionism he became highly respected in the field of automobile and aeronautical engineering. He believed in improving a successful product rather than taking a risk with a new invention. This philosophy of pursuing excellence is observed in Rolls-Royce even today. His motto, "Whatever is rightly done—however humble—is noble," is still followed at the company.

Rick Rubin

BIRTH NAME Frederick Jay Rubin
BORN March 10, 1963
DROPPED OUT New York University

Rick Rubin is the co-founder of Def Jam Records, a trend setting label for hip-hop, rap and rock music. Rubin's passion in life is music; it is through music that he deciphers everything in the world. Often described as an enigma, he connects with people through his love for music.

Rubin was born on Long Island and grew up listening to the Beatles. Graduating from high school in 1981, he entered New York University and while he was there founded the Def Jam record label with Russell Simmons in 1984. Some of their early releases included bands like LL Cool J, Public Enemy, Beastie Boys and Run DMC. Def Jam's records usually combined rap and heavy rock.

Rubin and Simmons parted ways in 1988, with the latter heading Def Jam in New York and Rubin moving to Los Angeles to start the Def American label. He went on to sign several heavy rock bands, including Slayer, Danzig, Masters of Reality, The Cult and Wolfsbane. He also signed The Jesus & Mary Chain and the stand-up comedian Andrew Dice Clay.

One of Rubin's most successful ventures was producing the breakthrough album of the Red Hot Chili Peppers, *Blood Sugar Sex Magik*. Rubin had close ties with rap artists also, signing the Geto Boys and carried on working with Public Enemy and LL Cool J. He encouraged collaboration between Aerosmith and Run DMC to produce their trendsetting song *Walk This Way*.

Signaling a new era in his career, Rubin renamed his company American Recordings, removing the word Def, for which he held a symbolic funeral. The first project under the new banner was Johnny Cash's *American Recordings*, in 1994, which was instrumental in reviving Johnny Cash's flagging career. Rubin also produced records for a number of older artists such as Tom Petty, Donovan and Neil Diamond.

In 2003, Rubin launched Mars Volta, a progressive rock group, with their album *De-Loused in the Comatorium*, giving his company, too, a new direction. In the same year, Rubin made the track *99 Problems* for Jay Z's *The Black Album*, for which he also appeared in the video. He produced Slipknot's hugely successful *Vol. 3 (The Subliminal Verses)*. Some of his other projects include System of a Down's *Mezmerize*, with Daron Malakian, Weezer's *Make Believe*, Shakira's *Oral Fixation 1&2* and Audioslave's *Out of Exile*.

It is Rubin's love for music that enables him to recognize good music long before it becomes popular and before actually making the tracks in the recording studio. Not particularly fond of working in the studio, he considers recording a process of bringing to life what is already in his head. He likens it to the notion of sculpture as a process of seeing the work in the block of stone and chipping away all the other parts to reveal the figure. He revels in being a true artist, letting his imagination flow to create unique music.

Rubin was instrumental in the rise of hip-hop music, lending his style of merging rap and heavy metal to several records in the pre-gangsta era. He is famous for always being ahead of the curve and knowing where the music industry is headed.

The recent proliferation of artists and the excessive importance given to producers is something that upsets Rick Rubin. With the competition increasing among artists, the emphasis has shifted from artist to song and from lyrics to promotion. To a music lover like Rubin, this trend is not a positive one, for he believes in the power of words and music, in experimenting with different styles and above all in entertaining people.

Harland Sanders

BIRTH NAME   Harland David Sanders
BORN   November 9, 1890
DIED   December 16, 1980
DROPPED OUT   Middle School

HARLAND SANDERS IS the entrepreneur behind the "finger lickin' good" Kentucky Fried Chicken (KFC) chain of fast food restaurants. A pioneer in the fast food business, he combined his love for cooking with his shrewd business acumen to start what is today the world's largest restaurant company.

Harland Sanders was born in Henryville, Indiana. His father Wilbert Sanders was a butcher. When Harland was six, his father died. His mother, Margaret Dunlevy Sanders, was forced to work in a factory, leaving Harland to take care of his three-year-old brother and baby sister. Those were tough days. His mother used to sew at night to make some money. Left to cook at home, Harland soon learned to cook a variety of dishes. By the age of seven, he had almost mastered the art.

When Harland was in sixth grade, he had to drop out of school to work full time. He worked on a farm near his house for two dollars a month to support his family. When he was 12, his mother married a produce farmer and moved to suburban Indianapolis. Harland left for a job on a farm in Greenwood, Indiana. At 15, he worked as a streetcar conductor. At 16, he was a private in Cuba. He took up various odd jobs, working as a steamboat ferry operator, firefighter and insurance salesman. He sold tires and operated a service station.

When he was 40, Sanders started making chicken for people who passed by his service station in Corbin, Kentucky. He had no restaurant and no tables either, but he served his customers on a dining table in his own living quarters. His new business attracted crowds and he soon moved to a restaurant across the street. He developed

Founder, Harland Sanders

his blend of 11 herbs and spices that are used today to season chicken at KFC restaurants worldwide. He perfected his technique of using a pressure cooker instead of pan-frying, thus reducing the cooking time. In recognition of his contribution to the state's cuisine, Governor Ruby Laffoon made him a Kentucky Colonel in 1935.

In the early 1950s, Colonel Sanders closed his business when Interstate 75 bypassed Corbin. Living on $105 a month in Social Security payments, he traveled by car across the country developing his franchise business. He got a nickel for each chicken sold in those restaurants. By 1964, he had over 600 chicken outlets in the U.S. and Canada. His became one of the most recognizable faces in the U.S.

He later sold the company for $2 million to a group of investors. The company went public in 1966 and was listed on the New York Stock Exchange in 1969. Heublein Inc. acquired it in 1971 for $285 million. In 1986, it was sold to R. J. Reynolds, who again sold it to PepsiCo for $840 million. KFC, Taco Bell and Pizza Hut were all brought under Tricon Global Restaurants Inc. by PepsiCo, which later sought shareholders' approval to change the name to Yum! Brands. The company now owns A&W All-American Food Restaurants, KFC, Long John Silvers, Pizza Hut and Taco Bell restaurants. It is the world's largest restaurant company.

Colonel Harland Sanders died in 1980 at the age of 90. His passion for cooking and his ability to fight the odds made him a successful entrepreneur.

David Sarnoff

BIRTH NAME David Sarnoff
BORN February 27, 1891
DIED December 12, 1971
DROPPED OUT High School

A VISIONARY WHO foresaw the huge potential of radio and television broadcasting, David Sarnoff led the Radio Corporation of America (RCA) from 1919 to 1970.

David Sarnoff was born in Uzlian, Russia. His father Abraham Leah Sarnoff was a painter. When David was five, his father moved to the U.S. to earn more money. David was sent to his great uncle's home to study the Talmud, the compilation of Jewish teachings. He led a disciplined life memorizing the sacred text.

In 1900, Abraham Sarnoff moved the whole family to the U.S. David learned that his father's health was failing and that his father was working very hard to make a living. David was only nine at the time, but he decided to work to support his family.

He began selling Yiddish-language newspapers in New York City, picking up bundles of newspaper as early as 4 AM in order to beat the competition from other delivery boys. He also earned some extra income singing in his synagogue. As he had very little time to study, he started taking English classes at the Educational Alliance. He learned enough English to read the newspaper and learned some business skills as well. He set up a newspaper stand when he was 14. He could not continue in high school as he had to work full-time to take care of his family.

Sarnoff got a job as an office boy for the Marconi Wireless Telegraph Company, becoming a junior operator in 1908. He advanced quickly in the company, always finding a way to be at the right place at the right time to meet and impress the people who could advance his career, including Marconi himself on his visits to the New York office.

Founder, David Sarnoff

Sarnoff moved quickly up the ladder at Marconi. In 1915, he suggested that the company develop a radio music box. His dream was to bring music to the homes of America. With World War I in progress, his plans were put on hold. After the war, Marconi's U.S. assets were absorbed into General Electric and the Radio Corporation of America (RCA) was spun off.

Sarnoff promoted the idea of creating broadcast programming to give people a reason to buy radio receivers. The Jack Dempsey–Georges Carpentier prizefight was the first special event broadcast. Radio sales soared and in three years, though a radio cost $75, sales reached $83.5 million. Sarnoff's next move was to create a national network for broadcasting. In 1926, as the general manager of RCA, he started the National Broadcasting Company (NBC). He was eager to introduce television as well, hoping to supply "sight with sound." Sarnoff predicted that television would become an important factor in America's economy. In 1939, at the New York World Fair, television was introduced. World War II hampered the growth of television; but, after the war, RCA introduced television in a big way and eventually RCA set color TV standards for all American broadcasters.

David Sarnoff retired in 1970 and died a year later in his sleep. With his keen foresight and great determination, he brought about a revolution in the broadcasting industry.

Vidal Sassoon

BIRTH NAME Vidal Sassoon
BORN January 17, 1928
DROPPED OUT Elementary School

VIDAL SASSOON'S CHAIN of hair salons is known worldwide for its wide range of hair products and chic hairstyles. In the mid-1960s, he created hairstyles like the wash-and-wear perm and the hugely popular classic bob cut.

Sassoon was born in the East End of London and had a tough childhood. Vidal's father left home when he was five; he and his little brother spent six years in an orphanage. The family was reunited only after his mother married again and took her children with her.

When Sassoon was 14, his mother had a dream in which she saw him in a barbershop. Although he wanted to be a football player, his mother felt that he should seek a profession in order to earn some money. She took him to Adolph Cohen's Beauty and Barber Shop in the East End, where he began his initial training. He decided that if he had to become a hairstylist, he might as well become the best in the industry.

Sassoon soon realized that his cockney accent was taking him nowhere. He wanted to join the stylish and posh West End salons, but realized that he had to learn to speak proper English in order to do that. He started going to the theatre in the evenings to learn proper English. He spent a lot of time listening and voice training.

Influenced by his mother, who was politically active and had joined the anti-Fascist movement, Sassoon took an active part in the movement. Putting his career on hold in 1948, he left London to join Israel's War of Independence. He wanted to stay on, join the university and become an architect but was forced to return to London because his family was poor and needed his support.

In 1960, Sassoon returned to London and opened a salon on Bond Street in Mayfair. He worked hard and perfected new techniques to get simple and elegant styles. He soon became famous for his innovative cuts and began to be known as the "founder of modern hairdressing."

His method of haircutting became popularly known as "Sassooning"; models, film stars and other celebrities started sporting his hairstyles. The 60s in Britain was a time of creativity. Sassoon's association with fashion designer Mary Quant made him even more popular. His $5,000 haircut to create an elfin look for Mia Farrow on the sets of the horror film Rosemary's Baby made headlines everywhere.

Sassoon has authored two bestselling books and has hosted his own TV show. Many successful hairstylists have trained in his schools and he has a huge range of hair care products that are known worldwide.

Although Vidal Sassoon could not attend regular school and had to drop out early in order to earn a living, his determination to be the best helped him leave a lasting impression in the world of fashion.

Millionaire Dropouts Trivia

Four out of five of America's richest people are dropouts:
number 1, Bill Gates, worth $50 billion;
number 3, Paul Allen, worth $22 billion;
number 4, Michael Dell, worth $17.1 billion;
number 5, Sheldon Adelson, worth $6.1 billion.

Dave Thomas

BIRTH NAME David Thomas
BORN February 7, 1932
DIED January 8, 2002
DROPPED OUT High School

Dave Thomas was a pioneer in the restaurant business. He founded the Wendy's Old Fashioned Hamburgers chain.

Dave Thomas was born in Atlantic City, New Jersey, to a single mother. When he was only six weeks old, he was adopted by Rex and Auleva Thomas. He was barely five years old when Auleva Thomas died of rheumatic fever and young Dave Thomas spent his childhood years moving from place to place as his adoptive father Rex went looking for jobs. A memorable part of Dave's childhood was the time he spent with his grandmother in Michigan. Dave's emphasis on respect for people and maintaining excellent quality of service were values he learned from her.

Thomas started working at 12, as a counterman at a restaurant in Knoxville. He loved the restaurant business so much that he always dreamt of opening a hamburger restaurant. When he was 15, he dropped out of school and worked at the Hobby House Restaurant in Ft. Wayne. It was here that he met Colonel Sanders, founder of Kentucky Fried Chicken, who was a major source of inspiration and influence in his life. He helped restore four KFC units that were not doing well and sold them back to KFC, becoming a millionaire at 35.

In 1969, Thomas's dream to open a restaurant of his own came true when he started the Wendy's Old Fashioned Hamburger restaurant in Columbus, Ohio, naming the chain after his young daughter. He wanted the restaurant to be a place where families could enjoy made-to-order, hot-off-the-grill sandwiches and fresh beef hamburgers that are square rather than round. He always said, "At Wendy's we don't cut corners!" The restaurant became such a success that Thomas received a number of awards and honors. He became a pioneer in the fast food industry and a role model for managers in the restaurant business.

Adoption was an issue that was very close to Dave's heart, having been an adopted child himself. He wanted to see that every child had a permanent home. When he was asked to head the White House Initiative on Adoption in 1990, he found that there were many obstacles to adoption. In 1992, he started the Dave Thomas Foundation for Adoption, a not-for-profit organization. His initiative helped in the passing of two bills—a one-time tax credit of $5,000 for adoptive parents, and the Adoption and Safe Families Act. The two bills helped in making the adoption process easier and more affordable. The foundation also worked with the U.S. Postal Service to bring out a colorful 33-cent adoption postage stamp that said, "Adopting a Child, Shaping a Life, Building a Home, Creating a World."

Thomas funded the Gordon Teter Chair for Pediatric Cancer Research, the Dave Thomas Family Primary Care Center and The Dave and Lorraine Thomas Clinical Laboratory at the Children's Hospital in Columbus. He established a number of educational centers and programs. Always haunted by the fact that he had dropped out of school, he went back to school 45 years later and got his GED from Coconut Creek High School in Ft Lauderdale. He considered this one of his greatest achievements. Although he was an extraordinarily successful businessman, he considered his family—his wife Lorraine, his five children and 16 grandchildren—his biggest accomplishment.

The Wendy's TV commercials with Thomas as the Wendy's spokesman, made him the most recognizable face in America; and people loved him for his down-to-earth, simple style. The campaign made it into the Guinness World Records as the longest running television advertising campaign starring a company founder.

When Thomas died in 2002, at 69, from cancer of the liver, he had become an American folk hero who used his heart and his millions to create a better world.

Kemmons Wilson

BIRTH NAME Charles Kemmons Wilson
BORN January 5, 1913
DIED February 12, 2003
DROPPED OUT High School

Kemmons Wilson founded the Holiday Inn hotel chain. He started out with the dream of providing tourists comfortable, clean and affordable lodging. He ended up revolutionizing the lodging industry worldwide.

Kemmons Wilson was born in Osceola, Arkansas. His father was an insurance salesman who died when Kemmons was nine months old. His mother, Ruby "Doll" Wilson, moved to Memphis, Tennessee, where she got a job as a dental assistant. Kemmons grew up in Memphis under her guidance. When he was 14, he was delivering a bicycle to a store when a car hit him. It was believed at that time that he could never walk again, but he recovered with the help of his doctor, Willis Campbell.

When Wilson's mother lost her job during the Great Depression, he was forced to drop out of school and look for a job. With a loan of $50 from a friend, he set up a popcorn machine in a theatre lobby. In 1933, he bought a house for himself and his mother with the money he made. His mother drilled into his head that he could do anything he wanted to do and Wilson firmly believed that.

In 1951, Wilson was on vacation with his wife, his two sons and three daughters, when he was forced to pay two dollars extra for each child in a motel. He thought it unfair that the motels charged so much and did not even provide enough comforts for what they charged.

Wilson felt the traveling public deserved better and vowed to start a chain of motels that would provide clean, comfortable and affordable accommodation to tourists. His wife did not take him se-

Founder, Kemmons Wilson

riously at the time, but Wilson made notes, measured the rooms and came back to Memphis with enough information to start on his plan. Adopting the name Holiday Inn from an old Bing Crosby movie that his draftsman had seen, Wilson sketched out his design. The first Holiday Inn opened in August 1952. He made sure that his motels had air-conditioning, swimming pool and restaurant facilities. Most of all, he ensured that children were not charged extra. Holiday Inn went International in 1960. Today, there are many Holiday Inns across the U.S. and many more in other countries as well.

Wilson received a number of awards and honors. He it was inducted into the American Motel Magazine Hall of Fame in 1961; and he received the Golden Plate Award in 1965, the Horatio Alger Award in 1970 and the Northwood University Outstanding Business Leader Award in 1985. He was inducted into the International Franchise Association Hall of Fame in 1989. He has also received five honorary degrees.

In his autobiography, *Half Luck and Half Brains*, he shares his experience of how a high school dropout could become a successful entrepreneur. He died in Memphis in 2003.

Driven by self-belief and ambition, Kemmons Wilson achieved what he wanted to. He demonstrated to the world that if one is hard working and determined, nothing can come in the way of success.

Millionaire Dropouts Trivia

Dropouts include:
- **22 Knights**
- **10 Nobel laureates**
- **4 Pulitzer prize winners**
- **6 Olympic gold medal winners**
- **Winners of 84 Academy Awards**
- **13 Presidents of the United States**
- **30 Additional Academy Award nominees**
- **19 members of the Rock and Roll Hall of Fame**
- **11 members of the Country Music Hall of Fame**

www.MillionaireDropouts.com

Millionaire Dropouts Trivia

Many of the world's greatest inventions were developed by dropouts, including television, radio, airplanes, cars, motion pictures, the incandescent light bulb, the car stereo tape deck, the gas mask, the traffic signal, earmuffs, the game of basketball, the sewing machine—and many more.

Inventors

Thomas Edison

BIRTH NAME Thomas Alva Edison
BORN February 11, 1847
DIED October 18, 1931
DROPPED OUT Elementary School

Thomas Alva Edison was born in Milan, Ohio, the youngest of Samuel and Nancy Edison's seven children. The family moved to Port Huron, Michigan when Al, as he was then called, was seven. He got a late start in school, and the three months he spent in the educational system did not go well, with his teacher describing him as "addled." His mother, being a teacher herself, decided to school him at home. Al learned most of his lessons from the R.G. Parker's book, School of Natural Philosophy.

At 13, Edison started selling newspapers and candy on a train, setting up a lab and a printing press in a baggage car and publishing the first newspaper ever printed on a train. When he was 16, he saved a little boy named Jimmie from being hit by a runaway railcar. Jimmie's father was so grateful that he took Edison under his wing and trained him to be a telegraph operator. Edison was partially deaf and hence not easily distracted by the operator next to him or other outside noise.

The rapid expansion of the telegraph industry in the late nineteenth century offered a number of opportunities and Edison traveled from place to place within the United States in the years 1863–1868, taking telegraph jobs and continuing his experiments. He ended in Boston in 1868, working for Western Union and working on his inventions. He quit at the beginning of 1869, at 22, to become a full-time inventor. He patented an electric vote recorder, a commercial failure; and Edison resolved that he would invent only things that people found useful. In 1869, he moved to New York and continued experimenting with telegraphy, inventing, among other things, the Universal

Inventor, Thomas Edison

Stock Printer, the first electricity-based broadcast system. With the $40,000 he earned for this and related inventions, he set up a small laboratory in Newark, New Jersey. In 1876, he set up his research laboratory in Menlo Park, New Jersey, where his staff could work on many inventions at once. This was really the first laboratory devoted to research and development of practical products, and the lab itself may be Edison's greatest invention. While he continued to experiment, his primary role was in supervising and directing the work of others, many of them better trained and more scientifically inclined than Edison himself.

In 1877, Edison invented his first phonograph. Sound was recorded on tin foil cylinders in the machine and then reproduced. He toured the country promoting the device for use as a dictation machine and was invited to the White House to show the phonograph to President Rutherford B. Hayes in 1878. It would be nearly a decade later before Edison took an interest in recorded music discs for home entertainment.

The bulk of Edison's patents, whether they pertained to the telegraph, the telephone or the electric light, were for improvements to technologies others had invented. Edison, though, did invent the first motion picture camera, along with a system to view the films.

Edison famously improved the light bulb after purchasing the patent from Henry Woodward and Mathew Evans. He applied his trial-and-error process to finding a long-lasting filament material and went on to manufacture light bulbs and demonstrate them in cities around the world. He then went on to become one of the pioneers of the electrical generation and transmission industry.

Thomas Alva Edison, "the wizard of Menlo Park," as one newspaper reporter dubbed him, is the world's most famous inventor of all time. February 11, Edison's birthday, is celebrated as National Inventors' Day in America. With his technological and organizational innovations, Thomas Alva Edison proved his teacher wrong and revolutionized the way we live in this world.

Florence Melton

BIRTH NAME Florence Spurgeon
BORN November 6, 1911
DROPPED OUT Elementary School

Born in Philadelphia, Florence Spurgeon grew up in a family that stressed the importance of charity not just for recognition, but as a means of rendering genuine help to mankind. Florence was greatly influenced by her grandmother, who taught her Jewish values and inspired her to be a loving and caring human being.

Soon after moving to Columbus, Ohio, in the early 1940s, Florence, now married to Aaron Zacks, served on the Board of United Way and the Red Cross Nutrition Corps. She also served on the board of the Huntington National Bank, becoming the first woman to do so; and she was a founding member of the Coalition for the Advancement of Jewish Education (CAJE).

On a trip to visit the Firestone Tire and Rubber Company in Akron, in 1947, Mrs. Zacks saw a piece of foam latex, a material Firestone had developed during World War II. The company was searching for ideas to use the material. Mrs. Zacks came up with the idea of making a slipper out of it. She stitched up a soft, washable, foam-soled slipper and quickly sold a lot of them.

Later that same year, Mrs. Zacks, her husband and a partner started the R.G. Barry Corporation to manufacture the new Angel Treads Slippers. R.G. Barry became the largest manufacturer of comfort footwear in the world.

After her first husband's death, Mrs. Zacks married industrialist and philanthropist Samuel M Melton in 1968. With his support, she launched a novel method to promote Jewish education. Always having been passionate about it, she started the Florence Melton Adult Mini-School, together with her husband and the Hebrew University of Jerusalem.

Inventor, Florence Melton

The school offers a two-year program and introduces adult learners to the complexity, depth and beauty of the Jewish heritage. Mrs. Melton has been actively involved in the Mini-School, first as chairperson of the board and later as chairperson emerita. With her guidance, the school has evolved and begun to grow in new directions. These adult mini-schools have over 6,000 students, 17,000 alumni and a faculty of over 300 in more than 60 cities across the globe.

Mrs. Melton's passion for Jewish education has been such that she has served on various committees and commissions both locally and internationally. In recognition of her good work, she has been given numerous honorary degrees and awards.

Mrs. Melton has a creative side to her, too, writing poetry, plays and music; and in 1994, at 82, she became a Bat Mitzvah at Congregation Tifereth Israel.

Florence Melton has not merely been a successful entrepreneur and innovator. Her dedication and sense of service has made her a truly successful human being as well.

Millionaire Dropouts Trivia

A member of the all-time top selling band The Beatles, George Harrison, was a dropout.

Earl Muntz

BIRTH NAME Earl Muntz
BORN 1914(?)
DIED June 20, 1987
DROPPED OUT High School

Earl Muntz was born in Elgin, Illinois. As a small boy he loved playing with gadgets. He built his own radio at 8 and one of the first car radios anywhere at 14. He started selling used cars when he was 20; his mother had to sign all the paperwork, as he wasn't old enough yet.

In 1941, Muntz moved to Glendale, California, and opened a used car lot, followed by another in Los Angeles. He signed up adman Mike Shore, who devised gimmicks that made Muntz the largest used car seller in the country. They pitched "Madman Muntz," and his crazy prices, but Muntz was crazy as a fox, buying used cars in the Midwest, paying servicemen $50 apiece to drive the cars west, and selling the cars for twice what he paid.

Muntz went from selling cars cheap to selling cheap TVs. He was a high school dropout, but he had more common sense than the engineers he hired to design televisions. His cost-cutting technique—snipping out one component after another with the wire cutters he carried in his shirt pocket until a circuit quit working, then telling the engineer to add back that one component—became known as "muntzing." His barebones circuitry made for a television that only worked well in urban areas with a strong broadcast signal; but that's where the market was and he was able to compete with the major brands. He was able to get televisions down below $200 retail for the first time and eventually produced a model that broke the $100 barrier, selling for $99.95. He promoted his low-cost sets with heavy advertising, including skywriting over major cities. It was Muntz's skywriting—paid for by the letter—that popularized the abbreviation *TV* for *television*.

Muntz leveraged his nationwide reputation to introduce the first American-built sports car, the Muntz Jet. He bought the design rights to an aluminum-body two-seat sports car initially developed by an Indy 500 race car designer, Frank Kurtis. Kurtis had built fewer than 20 cars and was no marketer. Muntz added a rear seat on a longer wheelbase, replaced the aluminum sheet metal with steel, put in a bigger engine, and proceeded to lose a thousand dollars on every car he sold. It was the only business he started that he never made money on. Today the cars, of which fewer than 500 were built, are collector's items worth more than 10 times their original selling price of $5,500.

The advent of color television forced Muntz's cheap black and white sets off the market, and Muntz went bankrupt, losing millions. But he went on to apply his particular brand of innovation to automotive sound systems, harking back to his tinkering as a boy. He invented the four-track car stereo, precursor to the eight-track system that would become a standard car accessory for two decades. He licensed music from the major record labels and sold four-track tapes for his installed base.

Muntz kept going from business to business until his death in 1987, at 73. Earl Muntz's passion for machines and new technology, combined with his innovative marketing strategy made him one of the best known and most successful inventors and retailers of his time.

Isaac Merrit Singer

BIRTH NAME Isaac Merrit Singer
BORN October 27, 1811
DIED July 23, 1875
DROPPED OUT Middle School

ISAAC MERRIT SINGER was born near Pittstown, New York. When he was 10, his parents got divorced. His father remarried, and Isaac didn't get along with his stepmother. When he was 12, he moved to Oswego, New York, to stay with his older brother, working in his brother's machine shop as an apprentice.

When he was 19, Singer worked for a few months as a machinist but left to join a touring troupe of actors. The same year, he married for the first time and settled in New York City for a few years before returning to upstate New York, this time in the Cooperstown area, to work in another machine shop.

Singer continued to alternate among being a machinist, being an actor, and being a groom (not always remembering to get divorced first). He received his first patent in 1839, for a rock-drilling machine. He sold the patent for $2,000 and used the money to form the Merritt Players. After five years, the troupe disbanded because of financial losses, and Singer took a job in a print shop in Fredericksburg, Ohio, where the troupe was when it broke up. There he came up with an idea for a machine to cut wood blocks used in printing. He moved to Pittsburgh and then back to New York City, where he built a prototype of the machine. When that prototype was destroyed in a boiler explosion, a machinist who had heard about the machine, Orson Phelps, invited Singer to Boston to recreate it

Working in the Phelps shop, where the wood cutting machine eventually turned out to be unsuccessful, Singer took a look at some Lerow and Blodgett sewing machines. He quickly found a way to improve them, making them much more reliable, easier to manufac-

Inventor, Isaac Merit Singer

ture and easier to use. He received a patent for his improved design in 1851, at 40.

Forming a partnership with George B Zieber and Phelps, Singer founded the Jenny Lind Sewing Machine Company, later changing the name to I.M. Singer & Co. Elias Howe had developed and patented a sewing machine in 1846; he and several other sewing machine manufacturers separately entered into a series of legal battles with Singer. These were resolved by the manufacturers agreeing to pool their patents instead of fighting in court. This agreement became the first patent pool that allowed production of complicated machines without legal battles over patent rights.

By late 1860s, Singer became the world's largest producer of sewing machines and Isaac Singer became a wealthy man. Singer's machines were designed for both domestic and commercial use. They were reliable, long lasting and, thanks to Singer's introduction of the installment credit plans, affordable.

In 1867, Singer established a factory in Scotland at Clydebank, near Glasgow, entering the European market. He later set up factories in Paris and Rio de Janeiro, making Singer the first American-based multinational corporation.

After Singer's death in 1875, his many children and many wives fought over his two wills to divide his estate of about $14,000,000 among them.

Isaac Merrit Singer used his creative energy to develop the world's first practical sewing machine and to start the first multinational company based in the United States.

Wilbur Wright & Orville Wright

BIRTH NAMES Wilbur Wright, Orville Wright
WILBUR: BORN April 16, 1867
DIED May 30, 1912
ORVILLE: BORN August 19, 1871
DIED January 30, 1948
DROPPED OUT High School

WILBUR WRIGHT WAS born in Millville, Indiana. Four years later, his brother Orville was born in Dayton, Ohio. Their father, Milton Wright was a minister in the Church of the United Brethren in Christ. The boys had a good childhood. Their father often bought them toys and other trinkets; When they were 7 and 11, he brought home a small flying toy that inspired their interest in flying. Some years later, the boys tried to build something similar to it. Calling their models bats, they discovered that the larger they were, the less they flew. When all attempts to make them fly failed, Orville and Wilbur returned to kite flying.

Wilbur was a good student and would have graduated from high school, had the family not moved during his senior year. Orville was only an average student and dropped out of school to start a printing company with his brother. Always tinkering with gadgets, the boys started repairing their friends' bicycles. In 1893, they set up a bicycle repair shop of their own and later went on to make and sell their own bicycles.

In 1896 the Wrights' interest in flying was rekindled when they read of the death of a French experimenter. They studied the available literature and engineering calculations related to both powered flight and gliding—or soaring—flight. Their interest was more in the latter, as it presented the interesting questions, they thought, relating to control of the flight path.

Inventors, Wilbur & Orville Wright

The Wright brothers carefully and methodically analyzed the problem of flight: managing propulsion, lift, and control, the last of which had largely been ignored by others. They checked and corrected published calculations. They built a wind tunnel and conducted hundreds of experiments with models. They built ever-larger gliders, experimenting with them at Kitty Hawk each year to be sure they understood how flight control worked before they attempted powered flight. Their major breakthrough, on top of all their other improvements, was understanding how to control the direction of flight by changing the shape of the wing. They accomplished this, with their lightweight wood and fabric wings, by physically bending the wing, using cables attached to levers. Today's giant passenger jets use flaps to accomplish the same thing.

In 1903 they returned to Kitty Hawk with a powered plane. They had designed and fabricated a propeller and engine, with a bicycle chain drive, of course. On December 17, at 10:35 AM, with Orville Wright at the controls, the first controlled, machine-powered, sustained flight took off; it lasted 12 seconds.

The Wrights continued to develop their design, using methods that would be familiar to any modern engineer, and obtained a patent for the Wright Flying Machine in 1906. Their planes became the world's first military airplanes and the two brothers impressed the whole world after successful demonstrations and exhibitions in France, Italy, Germany and the United States.

Neither brother ever married, their only passion being aviation. Wilbur Wright died at the age of 45 from typhoid. In 1932, a national monument was dedicated to the Wright brothers at Kitty Hawk. In 1948, at the age of 77, Orville Wright died of heart attack.

The Wright brothers' hard work and their passion for flying gave the world its first practical airplane and opened the skies for everyone.

Millionaire Dropouts Trivia

America's richest elementary school dropout, the late H.L. Hunt, was worth billions.

Powerful Dropouts

Powerful Dropouts

Powerful Dropouts

Powerful Dropouts

Powerful Dropouts

Powerful Dropouts

Powerful Dropouts

Powerful Dropouts

Powerful Dropouts

Mortimer J. Adler

BIRTH NAME Mortimer Jerome Adler
BORN December 28, 1902
DIED June 28, 2001
DROPPED OUT High School

MORTIMER J. ADLER was an education theorist, author and philosopher who advocated the study of philosophy for everyone and the need to apply it in every sphere of daily life. He is often considered a zealot for his single-minded pursuit of making the classics the basis of all education.

Adler was born in New York City, where his father was a jewelry salesman and his mother was a schoolteacher. He dropped out of high school at 14 to focus on his job as a copyboy at *The New York Sun*. Mortimer decided to take night classes at Columbia University to become a journalist. It was in these classes that he first read John Stuart Mill and became fascinated with philosophy. He resolved to read Plato and other philosophers to further his knowledge.

Adler received a scholarship from Columbia University for his undergraduate studies but was not awarded a degree, as he did not complete his physical education course, which he declared to be "a nuisance." He then joined the graduate program and impressed the faculty to such an extent that he was invited to join as staff while he was only a student. Adler received a Ph.D. even though he never got his undergraduate degree.

Adler became an advocate for the integration of science, literature and philosophy, stressing the need for philosophy to be practical more than theoretical. He wanted young people to gain knowledge through discussions and debates. He compiled a book, *Dialectic*, in 1927, in which he summarized the major philosophical and religious ideas of the western world. In 1952, Adler and Robert M. Hutchins edited *Great Books of the Western World*, a 54-volume set published by Encyclopedia Britannica.

Editor, Mortimer Adler

Adler's other important publications with Britannica were *Gateway to the Great Books, The Great Ideas Program* and T*he Annals of America.* In the *Propaedia* he outlined all human knowledge. All the while when he wrote, edited and published, Adler also taught first at Columbia University, then at the University of Chicago and the University of North Carolina. He also was on the board at Britannica and at The Ford Foundation.

Adler co-founded the Institute for Philosophical Research at the University of North Carolina, The Aspen Institute and The Center for the Study of The Great Ideas.

The works of Aristotle and St. Thomas Aquinas influenced Adler deeply. He believed in a liberal course of study with philosophy and arts as the basis of education. He thought students should not have to select vocational courses. He recognized the importance of education for three key reasons; to learn how to spend leisure time, how to make a living ethically and how to be a responsible citizen.

Adler tried to bring philosophy to the masses, so they could delve into a subject rather than just know it superficially. He strove to make his writing accessible to any reader, not just academics. Two of his most famous and influential books are *How to Read a Book* and *How to Think About War and Peace.*

Mortimer Adler died in June 2001 after successfully sowing the seed of philosophical interest in the minds of millions of young Americans. The world will remember him for his emphasis on making philosophy the foundation of all educational reform.

Jackie Collins

BIRTH NAME Jacqueline Jill Collins
BORN October 4, 1941
DROPPED OUT High School

JACKIE COLLINS, QUEEN of spirited, sexy novels based on celebrity lives, was born in London in 1941. She has one older sister, Joan, the Hollywood actress of *Dynasty* fame, and one younger brother, William. Her father, Joe Collins, was a theatrical agent and wanted both his daughters to join the theatre. Jackie's mother Elsa was a former dancer. Jackie started writing stories when she was eight years old, for her classmates, who were thrilled to read the steamy stories. Jackie was a playful girl, interested in entertaining others as well as having a good time herself.

Jackie Collins dropped out of school in her teens and her parents sent her to live in Los Angeles with Joan. On returning to England, Jackie married Wallace Austin in 1959. They were not happy together and, after the birth of their child Tracy, Wallace left Jackie and died soon after. Collins's second marriage was to Oscar Lerman, a nightclub and art gallery owner, with whom she had two daughters, Tiffany and Rory. The couple moved to Los Angeles so Collins could write books, surrounded by the world of movies and business, from which she took inspiration for her stories.

In 1968 Collins's first book, *The World is Full of Married Men*, equally shocked and delighted fans with her honest look at sexuality. The book was banned in Australia, giving Collins lots of media attention and making her successful overnight. She followed it up with more sensationalism, in Stud, in 1969, and the sequel *Bitch*, in 1979, focusing on the debauchery that came along with the glamour and high life of the movies. Her other books include *Sinners, The Love Killers, The World is Full of Divorced Women, Lovers and Gamblers, Chances* and the hugely successful *Hollywood Wives*, which was made into a miniseries starring Anthony Hopkins and Candice Bergen.

Author, Jackie Collins

Lucky and *Chances* were turned into a six-hour miniseries staring Nicolette Sheridan and Sandra Bullock. *Lady Boss* was made into a miniseries in 1992, and starred Kim Delaney. Collins also wrote the screenplay for *Yesterday's Hero*.

The sequel to *Chances*, *Lucky* also rose to number one on the *New York Times* bestseller list. *Hollywood Husbands* was about the lives of the men of Hollywood and kept everyone guessing the characters' true identities. In *Rock Star*, Collins told the story of three superstars of a rock band. In *Hollywood Kids*, she wrote about the power struggles, ambition, sex and drugs that the younger generation of Hollywood celebrities was entangled in. Her next book, *Vendetta*, published in 1996, again became a *New York Times* bestseller. *L.A. Connections, Dangerous Kiss, Lethal Seduction, Hollywood Wives: The New Generation* and *Deadly Seduction* also sold very well.

In 1998, Collins started her own show on television, *Jackie Collins Hollywood*, where she talked to a wide variety of stars.

Sometimes derided for being the queen of trash literature, Collins is an extremely successful novelist and has sold over 400 million copies of her books in over 40 countries.

Collins lives in Los Angeles and enjoys traveling to exotic places so she can include them in her books. She is also fond of photography and listening to soul music. Her husband died in the early 1990s after a long battle with cancer. Collins was devastated, but she continued with her work and spent time with her grandchildren. She has faced several personal losses through cancer and each time she has come out of it stronger. Jackie Collins is truly a survivor.

David Copperfield

BIRTH NAME David Seth Kotkin
BORN September 16, 1956
DROPPED OUT Fordham University

BORN IN METUCHEN, New Jersey, David Copperfield was passionate about magic from childhood. Learning card tricks from his grandfather, he started performing when he was 12. He became the youngest person ever admitted to the Society of American Magicians. At 16, he was teaching a course in magic at New York University.

Copperfield dropped out from Fordham University in New York to play the lead in an original musical, *The Magic Man*. His performance brought him instant fame and it went on to become the longest running musical ever staged in Chicago. ABC television, recognizing his talent, made him the host of the show *The Magic of ABC*. CBS then signed him for a series called *The Magic of David Copperfield*, where his mind-boggling illusions before a live audience catapulted him to fame. The show won several awards and David Copperfield became a household name.

Copperfield mesmerizes viewers with his vanishing acts. In 1983, he made the Statue of Liberty disappear. He walked through the Great Wall of China and escaped from Alcatraz. He is the first illusionist to fly without the use of wires. He once made 13 randomly selected people from the audience of a live show disappear.

Copperfield's illusions are enormously popular with audiences. As a result, he has become one of the highest paid entertainers in the world. Yet he considers his greatest achievement to be Project Magic, a rehabilitation program he developed to improve dexterity and motor skills in disabled patients using simple, sleight-of-hand magic. The project is in operation in over 1,000 hospitals and 30 countries across the world and has helped in motivating patients and building their self-esteem.

Copperfield's Broadway show *Dreams and Nightmares* broke box-office records. His shows in Europe, North and South America and Asia have been staged in front of packed audiences. He has also been featured in magazines such as *Vanity Fair, Esquire, Architectural Digest* and *Paris Match*. The Library of Congress has named him a living legend. The French government has conferred on him the title Chevalier of Arts and Letters. He also appears on the stamps of four countries. Madame Tussaud's, in London, has honored Copperfield by making a replica of him in wax. He is also the only living magician to receive a star on the Hollywood Walk of Fame.

The International Museum and Library of the Conjuring Arts in Nevada houses Copperfield's vast collection of props, books, documents and related products to the art of magic and its history.

David Copperfield, one of the greatest illusionists of all time, has changed the way the world looks at magic and transformed it into a new art form with his modern approach. He has reinvented the art of magic and taken it to new heights with his innovative and imaginative style. Blending mystery and romance to create spectacular illusions, he has become a legendary figure in the world of entertainment.

Millionaire Dropouts Trivia

Some of the highest-paid actors in the world (Tom Cruise, Tom Hanks, Jim Carrey, Johnny Depp and Leonardo Di Caprio) are all dropouts.

Simon Cowell

BIRTH NAME Simon Phillip Cowell
BORN October 7, 1959
DROPPED OUT High School

Simon Cowell is a music producer who rose to fame as a judge on the popular television programs *Pop Idol* and *American Idol*. His honest and often blunt assessment of contestants on the show made him a controversial but hugely successful judge.

Born in Brighton, England, the first time Cowell made a critical remark, according to his book *I Don't Mean to be Rude, But ...* , was at the tender age of four, when he looked at his mother's white fuzzy pillbox hat and said, "Mum, you look like a poodle." He dropped out of school when he was 16 and took a job in the mailroom at EMI Music Publishing, where his father, Eric Cowell, worked. The younger Cowell worked hard, eventually becoming a music producer, as he had an ear for music. He had a knack for identifying potential hits. BMG Records recognized his aptitude and took him on as an artists and repertoire (A&R) consultant in 1989.

Cowell became the man behind several pop success stories. He pioneered the emergence of famous bands like *Five* and *Westlife* and TV hits like cartoon puppets *Zig & Zag* and *The Teletubbies*. He claims that his biggest success was promoting the well-known pop-duo Robson and Jerome who hold the record for three consecutive number one singles on debut. By keenly following current trends and identifying talent, Cowell can today boast of sales of over 25 million albums, over 70 top-30 records and 17 number 1 singles.

When the TV series *Popstars* became a success, Cowell, along with Simon Fuller, decided to produce a musical talent show where the public would decide who should win. Auditions for the show numbered 10,000, becoming the most extensive auditions ever staged. The interactive nature of *Pop Idol* made it a popular show; the public watched and voted every Saturday evening. The final winner, Will

Producer, Simon Cowell

Young, got 4.6 million votes. The runner-up, Gareth Gates, got 4.1 million votes. Will Young's debut album *Evergreen/Anything is Possible* broke records as well as registering sales worth over $2 million. Gareth Gates' album, with sales of 1 million records, became a fast selling debut album.

Cowell became a celebrity, too, and the *Sunday Times* Rich List estimated that he earned $33.5 million in just a year, following the success of the *Pop Idol*. *American Idol*, the U.S. version of the show, was also an incredible success. The show's host was Ryan Seacrest. Performers Kelly Clarkson, Clay Aiken and Ruben Studdard became stars overnight. The panel of judges, which included Cowell, Paula Abdul and Randy Jackson, came to be loved by the audiences; by the end of the first season, Cowell got a contract that made him the highest paid judge on the panel.

The ability to recognize and promote potential talent has made Simon Cowell a successful producer, judge and promoter of TV shows and music albums. He has proved that everybody stands to gain when there's rich artistic talent waiting to be tapped.

Millionaire Dropouts Trivia

Some of the highest-paid actresses in the world (Cameron Diaz, Nicole Kidman, Angelina Jolie and Drew Barrymore) are all dropouts.

Dale Earnhardt

BIRTH NAME Ralph Dale Earnhardt
BORN April 29, 1951
DIED February 18, 2001
DROPPED OUT High School

DALE EARNHARDT WAS born in Kannapolis, North Carolina, into a racing family. His father, Ralph, was a successful driver who died of a heart attack in 1973 while working on his race car. Dale dropped out of high school in the ninth grade to focus on a career in cars and racing. As a teenager, to earn money he started racing hobby-class cars at night and worked making improvements on them during the day.

In 1975, Earnhardt began his career in stock car racing, driving for Ed Negre and later for Rod Osterlund. When the latter's regular driver, Dave Marcis, left to start his own team in 1979, Osterlund selected Earnhardt to race in the Winston Cup. He won the Rookie of the Year Award at the competition. It was the turning point of his career.

In 1981, Rod Osterlund sold his team to Richard Childress. Earnhardt and Childress formed a good partnership. They were determined to win the Winston Cup Championship conducted by the National Association of Stock Car Automobile Racing (NASCAR). Their first success was in 1986 and from then on; the triumphs came one after another, with Earnhardt accumulating six titles over nine seasons. He won the prestigious Daytona 500 on his twentieth attempt in 1998. He was also included in the list of 50 greatest drivers in NASCAR history, along with his father.

Earnhardt's aggressive driving style earned him the nickname The Intimidator. His style on the racetrack was just part of his winning strategy, not an indication of who he was as a person. To Earnhardt, success was everything. He said "second place is the first loser."

Stock Car Driver, Dale Earnhardt

Earnhardt was an innovative driver. In addition to being excellent at drafting, which exploits the fact two cars that are lined up and closely spaced go faster than a single car, he created a variation called side-drafting.

Winning seven NASCAR championships in his career, Earnhardt had total prize winnings exceeding $41 million. An estimated 40–50 percent of the memorabilia sold at NASCAR races was Earnhardt's. He drove the number 3 car for almost his entire career, sponsored first by Wrangler Jeans and later by GM Goodwrench.

Off the track, Earnhardt was a private person who enjoyed working on his Kannapolis farm. He was generous by nature and was involved in charitable work. He was married three times and had four children. His sons Kerry and Dale Jr. follow the family tradition of racing.

Dale Earnhardt died in a crash on the final lap of the 2001 Daytona 500, shocking fans across the country. Earnhardt was one of the most dashing sportsmen on the car racing tracks in the U.S. He played an important role in making stock car racing a national obsession in the country. His life is a blazing story of commitment and passion for a sport that revolves around speed.

Millionaire Dropouts Trivia

America's first billionaire, John D Rockefeller Sr., was high school dropout.

Albert Einstein

BIRTH NAME Albert Einstein
BORN March 14, 1879
DIED April 18, 1955
DROPPED OUT Luitpold Gymnasium

Albert Einstein was born in Ulm, Germany, and grew up in Munich, studying at the Luitpold Gymnasium. In 1894, his family moved to Pavia, Italy, while Albert remained in Munich to attend school. He dropped out after a term to join his family and eventually earned his secondary school diploma from Aarau, Switzerland in 1896.

On earning a teaching diploma from the Swiss Federal Institute of Technology (Eidgenössische Technische Hochschule) in Zurich, Einstein became a Swiss citizen. Unable to find a teaching position, he instead joined the Swiss Patent Office in 1902. While working there, Einstein earned his doctorate in 1905, the year now known as Annus Mirablis (Latin for year of wonders) because of the publication of four papers that revolutionized modern physics, all authored by Einstein. These papers, on Brownian motion, the photoelectric effect and special relativity, provided a theoretical basis to explain experimental results that had long baffled physicists. In one of the two special relativity papers he applied the equation $E = mc^2$ to the energy binding of the atomic nucleus for the first time.

Einstein preseted the theory of general relativity in a series of lectures 1915, replacing Newton's law of gravity with the Field Equation, which envisions gravity not as a force but rather as a consequence of the curvature of space–time. Einstein lived to see some experimental support for general relativity, but it was still controversial at his death. Today it is established fact, with its minute effects a necessary part of the calculations that allow the GPS system to remain accurate over time.

Physicist, Albert Einstein

From 1911 to 1914, Einstein was a professor at the University of Zurich, the University of Prague and then at ETH Zurich. He moved to Berlin in 1914 and after becoming a German citizen joined the Prussian Academy of Sciences. In 1921, he won the Nobel Prize for his paper on the photoelectric effect. He was the director of the Kaiser Wilhelm Institute for Physics until 1933.

Einstein's work was often discredited in Germany because of rising anti-Semitism; when Hitler came to power in 1933 Einstein renounced his German citizenship. He moved to Princeton, New Jersey, where he joined the Institute for Advanced Study and concentrated on the unification of the laws of physics. He became a U.S. citizen in 1940.

In his private life Einstein was a modest man who liked to sail and play the violin. He regarded himself a pacifist, except for the brief time during WW II when he instigated the Manhattan Project by writing to President Roosevelt urging the development of nuclear fission to counteract Hitler's plan of building the first atomic bomb. After the war, Einstein promoted the cause of international disarmament and was part of the World Government Movement. He was also a humanitarian and felt that Gandhi's views were the most enlightened of all the political men of his time.

Albert Einstein has become a pop culture icon in contemporary times and his name is a synonym for intelligence. He explored new frontiers of science with his endless curiosity and thirst for knowledge but always considered imagination to be more important than knowledge. Einstein is often acknowledged as the greatest scientist of the twentieth century. He propounded the theory of relativity and made important contributions to the growth of quantum mechanics, string theory and cosmology.

William Faulkner

BIRTH NAME William Falkner
BORN September 25, 1897
DIED July 6, 1962
DROPPED OUT High School

WILLIAM FAULKNER, NOBEL Prize–winning American author, was born William Falkner (without the *u*) in 1897 to Murry and Maud Butler Falkner in New Albany, Mississippi, the first of four sons. His great-grandfather Col. William Clark Falkner served in the Confederate Army, founded a railway and wrote a popular romantic novel.

Faulkner, the spelling he chose as an adult, set his novels in his native South. However, he joined the RAF in Canada, seeking military glory in World War I.

Although the war ended before he finished his training, Faulkner alluded to his being a war veteran. His time spent in training was fodder for his first novel, *Soldier's Pay*, written in 1925. Some of his most famous novels are *The Sound and the Fury*, *As I Lay Dying*, *Light in August*, *The Unvanquished*, *The Wild Palms*, *Absalom, Absalom!* and *Go Down, Moses*. Besides novels, Faulkner also wrote many short stories.

Faulkner entered the University of Mississippi, in Oxford, in 1919, even though he had not completed high school. As a student, Faulkner was involved in writing poems and short stories for the campus newspaper; he also founded *The Marionettes*, a dramatic club in the university. Faulkner dropped out of school again, in November 1920, after three semesters.

Faulkner's best known novel, *The Sound and the Fury*, was published in 1929. It was the story of an aristocratic southern family and its decline, narrated by four brothers.

Faulkner married his childhood friend Estelle Oldham in April 1929 after she divorced her first husband, Cornell Franklin. With her

Author, William Faulkner

two children, Malcolm and Victoria, they lived in Oxford. Faulkner, trying to increase his earnings and working nights at a power plant, wrote his masterpiece, *As I Lay Dying* in six weeks. He focused again on a family and the destiny of its members, but this time the characters were poor farm laborers.

In April 1930, *The Forum* published the short story "A Rose for Emily." That was followed by the publication of other stories in major magazines including *Collier's* and the *Saturday Evening Post*. Also in 1930, *Sanctuary*, which had earlier been rejected by publishers, was accepted and went on to become his best-selling novel at the time.

William and Estelle's first child, Alabama, born in 1931, survived only a few days. Deeply influenced by the loss, Faulkner wrote a collection of short stories *These 13*, and began on *Light in August*, a novel about race and how it affects relationships. In 1933 William and Estelle had a baby girl, Jill.

In 1936, Faulkner wrote *Absalom, Absolom!* He was elected to the National Institute of Arts and Letters in 1939. He was awarded the Nobel Prize for Literature for 1949 and Pulitzer Prizes for *A Fable* in 1955 and posthumously for *The Reivers*.

Faulkner was a writer-in-residence at the University of Virginia for several years. After a fall from his horse, Faulkner was taken to the hospital. He died of a heart attack in 1962 and was buried in St Peter's Cemetery in Oxford.

Tom Ford

BIRTH NAME Tom Ford
BORN August 27, 1961
DROPPED OUT High School

TOM FORD WAS born in Austin, Texas and grew up in Santa Fe, New Mexico. Interested in all aspects of design from an early age, Ford moved to New York when he was a teenager and enrolled in a course in art history at New York University. He switched to study interior design at the Parsons School of Design in New York, sudied there and at Parsons in Paris, finishing up in New York.

In 1986, he started working for designer Cathy Hardwick in New York and within two years became the Design Director at Perry Ellis. In 1990, Dawn Mello, Gucci's creative director, selected him to design ready-to-wear for its women's division, in Milan, and two years later Ford became design director at Gucci. He has been credited with turning around Gucci from a staid and stuck-in-the-rut brand to a fashion powerhouse by the late 1990s.

Taking a hands-on approach at Gucci, Ford created a particular style of clothing for the fashion house and worked to improve its brand. He upgraded the look and image of the company's store design and advertisements. Some of his advertisements received a lot of attention for their controversial content and depiction. Ford's marketing style started a craze for owning Gucci bags and other accessories covered with the Gucci logo, a type of presentation that has been copied by many other designers.

Under Ford's leadership, Gucci went on to acquire the Yves Saint Laurent label in 2000. Ford became the creative director for YSL, too. After ten productive years at Gucci, Ford decided to leave in 2004 to pursue his goal of directing films. He then announced that he would be designing his own fashion line.

Celebrities love Ford's sexy, sophisticated line of designer wear and they flaunt the Gucci label at many prestigious award functions.

Fashion Designer, Tom Ford

Each season the world waited with bated breath to see the new collection. The Council of Fashion Designers of America named Ford its designer of the year in 1995. His clients include Madonna, Bianca Jagger, Gwyneth Paltrow, Jennifer Lopez and Trudie Styler.

In May 2004, Ford joined Sothebys in Paris as an advisor. Meanwhile he is taking on acting and directing jobs in Hollywood.

Tom Ford is one of the most influential designers in the world of haute couture. He saved Gucci from the brink of bankruptcy and made it a thriving, vibrant brand by creating an elegant and sexy style that has become the favorite of celebrities. His emphasis on exploiting the power of a brand name to enhance image and sales has ushered in a new era for designers in the fashion world.

Millionaire Dropouts Trivia

The U.S. penny and quarter-dollar coins, as well as the one, five, twenty, one hundred and thousand-dollar bills all have images of dropouts.

Laird Hamilton

BIRTH NAME Laird John Zerfas
BORN March 2, 1964
DROPPED OUT High School

Laird Hamilton was born in San Francisco but grew up in Oahu, Hawaii, where he learned to surf. His adoptive father is the legendary Bill Hamilton, a big wave surfer of the 1960s. JoAnn Zyriek, Laird's mother, is also a surfer. Laird experienced racism in school, being the only blond-haired boy; for him the ocean became the place to even scores. Eventually he dropped out of school and moved to California, where he was able to fit in better. He even used his looks to his advantage by becoming a model.

Returning to Hawaii in the late 1980s, Hamilton made a statement with his innovative, powerful and aggressive style of surfing. To surf waves that were too big to catch by paddling he used jet skis and conquered a challenging spot on Maui called Peahi, now renamed Jaws. This area has become a favorite haunt for surfers keen to try out new big-wave surfing techniques.

Hamilton has been responsible for introducing several new styles of surfing. Using his tow-in surfing technique, which many of his peers considered cheating, he conquered the Teahupoo surf spot in Tahiti on August 17, 2000. This one act made him a legend in surfing circles and put him on the cover of Surfer magazine. The foil board technique, which combines hydrofoil technology with surfboards, is another innovation of his. Besides surfing, he excels in other water sports, including windsurfing, water skiing and jet skiing. Hamilton has played an important role in improving windsurfing techniques and increasing the popularity of the sport. He windsurfed between the Hawaiian islands of Oahu and Kauai in 2003, setting a speed record.

Hamilton's physical build has contributed in a big way to his success. At six-three, he can control the larger waves more easily than smaller surfers. can . He has been featured in several magazines and was named one of the 50 most beautiful people by People magazine in 1996.

Fame has taken Hamilton beyond the world of professional surfing. He has performed stunts for movies, including *Waterworld, Die Another Day, Night Waves, Totally Committed* and *Five Summer Stories*. He starred in North Shore, a movie about an unethical surfer. Besides acting and performing stunts, Hamilton provides expert advice to film and television companies on the technicalities of shooting in surf.

Hamilton excelled through his persistent experimentation with new methods of surfing. He has never been interested in entering competitions and views surfing as he does life, a challenge to master and then move on to new and bigger quests.

Laird Hamilton is the most celebrated big wave surfer in the world today. He is famous for his innovative methods and use of modern technology to push the limits of physical endurance and achieve breathtaking results.

Millionaire Dropouts Trivia

America's first millionaire, John Jacob Astor, was high school dropout.

William Hanna

BIRTH NAME William Denby Hanna
BORN July 14, 1910
DIED March 22, 2001
DROPPED OUT Compton Junior College

WILLIAM HANNA, CREATIVE force behind famous cartoons like Yogi Bear and Scooby Doo, was born in Melrose, New Mexico. His father was a construction supervisor for the Santa Fe Railway; so the family moved quite often. They finally settled in Los Angeles in 1919. William was a talented artist. He inherited his creative skills from the maternal side of the family, which included a number of writers who influenced William in his creative choices both in school and later. William joined The Boy Scouts in Los Angeles and was actively involved in the organization for the remainder of his life.

Hanna decided to become a structural engineer. He enrolled in Compton Junior College, majoring in engineering and journalism, but dropped out because of the Great Depression, working to help his father in the construction of the Pantages Theatre. In 1931, he joined the Harman-Ising cartoon studio, providing story and layout ideas to *Loony Tunes* and *Merrie Melodies*. In 1937, MGM decided to stop outsourcing its cartoon production and formed its own animation unit. Hanna shifted to MGM, becoming director for the *Captain and the Kids* series.

It was here that Hanna met Joseph Barbera and formed a long and successful partnership with him. They were most popular for their *Tom and Jerry* series, which won seven Academy Awards. Hanna and Barbera formed their own company, Hanna–Barbera Productions, in 1957, when MGM closed its animation production unit. They decided to focus on producing cartoons specifically for television, making some of the best-loved cartoon shows and creating characters like Huckleberry Hound, Yogi Bear, the Flintstones, Johnny Quest, the Banana Splits and Scooby Doo.

The Flintstones was the first half-hour animated sitcom on television and went on to become one of the world's most watched shows for the six years it aired. Hanna–Barbera Productions was the most successful television animation studio by the late 1960s.

The company also made animated films, including *A Man Called Flintstone,* in 1966, *Charlotte's Web,* in 1972 and *Heidi's Song,* in 1982. Hanna was an executive producer on *The Flintstones in Viva Rock Vegas,* in 2000, and for *Scooby Doo,* which was completed after his death.

Often referred to disparagingly as the poor man's Disney, the Hanna–Barbera collaboration led to the making of the some of the most memorable cartoon characters. Together they produced over 3000 cartoons. Hanna stayed actively involved with cartoons, even after selling Hanna–Barbera Productions to Taft Communications, co-producing *Once Upon a Forest.* One of the last hits of the company was *Dexter's Laboratory*.

William Hanna and Joseph Barbera received their star on the Hollywood Walk of Fame in 1976 and were inducted into the Television Academy Hall of Fame in 1983. Hanna married Violet Blanch Wogatzke in 1936; they had two children, a son, David, and a daughter, Bonnie. Hanna died in 2001 in Los Angeles. William Hanna was a successful man of his own making, relying on strong natural talents and turning whatever came his way into opportunity.

Harry Houdini

BIRTH NAME Erik Weisz
BORN March 24, 1874
DIED October 31, 1926
DROPPED OUT Elementary School

HARRY HOUDINI WAS born as Erik Weisz in Budapest, Hungary. His father, Mayer Samuel Weisz, was a religious scholar and teacher. The family went through hard times financially when he was young. His father moved first to Appleton, Wisconsin, where he served for a few years as a rabbi. Young Harry Weiss (the Americanized form of his Hungarian nickname Ehrie, and the spelling given the family's last name by an immigration clerk) left home at 12, hopping a freight train for Kansas City, hoping to earn money to help support the family. He worked at odd jobs and made his way east to New York City about a year later, in 1887, rejoining his family, who had moved there by then.

Harry started studying magic and took part in various athletic events, too. His idol was the father of the modern magic act, the French magician Robert Houdin, who had written *The Memoirs of Robert Houdin, Ambassador, Author, and Conjuror, Written by Himself.* Harry called himself Houdini when he started performing in public at 17.

Mayer Weiss died in 1892; Houdini was 18. He performed, first with his brother, at amusement parks and dime museums, replacing his brother in the act when he married Beatrice (Bess) Raymond, a singer. Initially specializing in card tricks, by 1895 they started introducing larger illusions, such as switching places in a trunk.

In 1899, Houdini met Martin Beck, a showman who encouraged him to focus on his escape act. Beck booked him on the Orpheum vaudeville circuit, leading to a tour of Europe. He returned to the U.S. famous for his escape tricks, freeing himself from handcuffs, chains and ropes. He staged public stunts everywhere he went, escaping from handcuffs provided by local police, jumping, manacled, off bridges, escaping from a milk can full of water. His most famous act, was the "Chinese water torture cell," in which he would dangle upside down in a locked glass cabinet full of water. He put in hours to perfect his stunts, holding his breath in a specially built tub to practice for his underwater acts.

After World War I, Houdini began a film career, acting first in a movie serial before starting his own film company in 1921. He acted in five more silent films, none of them commercial successes.

After the death of Houdini's mother in 1920, he started exposing people who claimed to be psychics and mediums, using his knowledge of stage magic to expose their tricks. He joined a committee of American scientists to protect people from being duped by such healers.

Houdini died tragically at 52. On a visit to McGill University, to give a lecture on spiritualism, he was asked if he could withstand a blow to the stomach. Before he could prepare by tightening his stomach muscles, a student hit him. He recovered from the blow but died of peritonitis from a ruptured appendix.

Houdini had made a pact with his wife Bess that he would contact her after death if possible and deliver a prearranged message. Bess held a séance for ten years every Halloween; but in 1936 she put out a candle beside Houdini's photograph, saying, "ten years is long enough to wait for any man."

Peter Jennings

BIRTH NAME   Peter Charles Archibald Ewart Jennings
BORN   July 29, 1938
DIED   August 7, 2005
DROPPED OUT   High School

PETER JENNINGS WAS born in Toronto, Ontario, Canada. His father, Charles Jennings, was head of the news department at the Canadian Broadcasting Corporation. When he was 9, Peter anchored a kids' show, *Peter's People*, for CBC Radio. He dropped out of high school and worked as a bank-teller and a disc jockey. Canada's first private TV network, CTV, noticed his coverage of a local train wreck and asked him to co-anchor its late-night *CTV National News*. He worked for CTV through 1964, covering the civil rights movement, the assassination of John F. Kennedy and other important events of the era. He joined ABC in 1965, anchoring *Peter Jennings with the News*. At 26, he was the youngest ever American network news anchor, but that worked against him, competing as he was against the mature and respected Walter Cronkite, Chet Huntley and David Brinkley. He lost the anchor slot in 1968.

Determined to make a comeback, Jennings stayed on at ABC as a foreign correspondent, covering the Middle East and the Lebanese civil war. After the Shah of Iran fled the country, Jennings was the first to get an interview with Iran's Ayatollah Khomeini. He also covered the massacre of Israeli athletes by Palestinian terrorists at the Munich Olympics. In 1978, he started anchoring *ABC World News Tonight* along with Frank Reynolds from Washington and Max Robinson from Chicago. From 1983 through April 2005, he was the sole anchor, covering major news events live as they unfolded. He spent more than 60 hours on the air following the attack on the World Trade Center on September 11, 2001. The coverage earned ABC News the Peabody and Dupont awards.

Journalist, Peter Jennings

Jennings was "in Berlin in the 1960s when the Berlin Wall was going up, and there again, in the late 1980s when it came down," according to his official ABC biography. Reporting from over 50 locations across the globe, he played a major role in covering the conflict in Bosnia, the war in Iraq, India–Pakistan relations, the crisis in Haiti and the drug trade in Central and South America. His *Peter Jennings Reporting* earned him several awards, including the 2004 Edward R. Murrow award for best documentary for *The Kennedy Assassination—Beyond Conspiracy*.

Over 175 million Americans watched *ABC 2000*, his coverage of Millennium Eve on December 31, 1999. It was the biggest live telecast ever. During his tenure as an anchor and senior editor of *World News Tonight*, his experience in the Middle East proved to be invaluable. ABC's coverage of the 1991 Gulf War and the 2003 War in Iraq greatly benefited by his experience and understanding of affairs in these countries. He also tackled several domestic issues like education, health care and tobacco. He received several major awards in his career, including 16 Emmys, two George Foster Peabody Awards and several Alfred I. Dupont–Columbia University Awards.

Jennings died in 2005 after battling lung cancer. ABC mourned his death with several special shows.

Peter Jennings ushered in a new era in television journalism, with his in-depth coverage of challenging and controversial issues.

Rosa Parks

BIRTH NAME Rosa Louise McCauley
BORN February 4, 1913
DIED October 24, 2005
DROPPED OUT Alabama State Teacher's College

ROSA MCCAULEY WAS born in Tuskegee, Alabama, to James and Leona McCauley, and grew up in Pine Level, Alabama, on her grandparents' farm. She entered the Montgomery Industrial School for Girls when she was 11 and later switched to the Alabama State Teacher's College for tenth and eleventh grades, only to drop out to care for her sick grandmother. The Montgomery Industrial School was founded by forward-thinking, liberal women who believed in the philosophy of self-worth. The education that she received here along with her mother's influence helped Rosa grow up strong, independent and fearless.

Rosa married Raymond Parks and they set up home in Montgomery, becoming members of the National Association for the Advancement of Colored People (NAACP), to help improve the conditions of African-Americans. She was actively involved in organizing voter registration drives in the city as well as in other civic and religious events. In 1943, Mrs. Parks was elected secretary of the Montgomery chapter of the NAACP.

In 1955 Mrs. Parks was working at a department store. She received worldwide attention for her refusal to vacate her seat on a public bus for a white passenger. She was arrested, tried and convicted for violating the local ordinance. Her act of civil disobedience triggered a boycott of all city buses that lasted over a year. Dr. Martin Luther King Jr. set up the Montgomery Improvement Association and rose to prominence due to his involvement in the boycott. In 1956, the Supreme Court overturned the Montgomery ordinance defining racial segregation as unconstitutional and outlawed segregation on public transportation.

Human Rights Activist, Rosa Parks

Mrs. Parks's act of disobedience stemmed from simply wanting to be treated with decency and dignity. It marked a turning point in the battle for racial equality by African-Americans and was the precursor to the emergence of Dr. Martin Luther King Jr. as a national leader of the civil rights movement.

Mrs. Parks lost her job as a result of her action and received constant death threats; the couple decided to move to Detroit in 1957. After struggling for eight years, Mrs. Parks got a job as an administrative assistant to U.S. Congressman John F. Conyers Jr., for whom she worked till 1987. She established the Rosa and Raymond Parks Institute for Self-Development to motivate the younger generation to achieve their goals.

During her lifetime, Mrs. Parks received several awards, including the Spingarn Medal in 1970, the Martin Luther King Jr. Award in 1980 and the Presidential Medal of Freedom in 1996. A road in Montgomery is named in her honor. Rosa Parks died on October 24, 2005 of natural causes in her Detroit home.

Mrs. Park's protest brought about dramatic changes in the rights of African-Americans in the South. A shy and quiet person, once she decided on something, she was determined to stand her ground and face the consequences with dignity and courage. A pioneer in the struggle for racial equality, Rosa Parks wished to be remembered as a person who "wanted to be free and wanted others to be free."

Sam Phillips

BIRTH NAME Samuel Cornelius Phillips
BORN January 5, 1923
DIED July 30, 2003
DROPPED OUT Coffee High School

SAM PHILLIPS WAS instrumental in the emergence of rock and roll music in the 1950s. He brought it to the mainstream and changed forever the world of music. Phillips launched several well-known artists, but the discovery that ensured his fame was Elvis Presley.

Phillips grew up in Florence, Alabama, on a cotton farm. Dropping out of Coffee High School to help support his mother and aunt in 1945, he moved to Memphis to work as a radio announcer and maintenance and broadcast engineer at WREC. Yearning to do more than just listen to music, he set up the Memphis Recording Service in January, 1950. In 1952 he formed Sun Records.

Phillips recorded rhythm and blues artists like James Cotton, Howlin' Wolf, Rosco Gordon, Little Milton and B. B. King from 1950 to 1954. The rhythm and blues genre consisted entirely of black musicians, but Phillips wanted to find a white singer who had a special sound. He found that singer in Elvis Presley, who came to the studio to record "My Happiness" and "That's When Your Heartaches Begin" as a gift for his mother's birthday. Recognizing instantly the emotional depth and variation in Presley's voice, Phillips decided to sign him and promote his career.

Presley's success opened the doors to thousands of hopeful singers. Some of Phillips's phenomenal success stories were Jerry Lee Lewis, Johnny Cash, Roy Orbison and Carl Perkins; but several others, such as Charlie Rich and Sonny Burgess were also successful. In 1955, because of severe financial strain, Phillips sold Elvis Presley's contract to RCA Records for $35,000.

Rock & Roll Pioneer, Sam Phillips

Phillips was able to bring together different streams of music, including blues, rhythm and blues, country and gospel, and provide musicians with a complete package from production to marketing. His studio's distinctive sound quality and the relaxed atmosphere of the recording sessions were its keys to success. Phillips was responsible for bringing out *Rocket 88* by Jackie Brenston and Ike Turner's Delta Cats band in 1951, which is widely credited as being the first rock and roll record.

His contribution to the music industry has been so singular that during his lifetime Phillips was inducted into the Rock and Roll Hall of Fame, the Alabama Music Hall of Fame and the Blues Hall of Fame. In 1991, he received a Grammy Trustees Award.

Besides his involvement in Sun Records, Phillips made a fortune in the hotel business, after he invested in the local Holiday Hotel, which eventually grew into the Holiday Inn chain. Phillips died of respiratory failure at Francis Hospital in Memphis in July 2003, at 80. Sam Phillips was a humble man and remained modest about his role as a pioneer in the rock and roll industry.

Millionaire Dropouts Trivia

Elijah McCoy, who invented the ironing board as well as a lubrication system for steam engines, was a dropout. He attracted notice among his African-American contemporaries.
Booker T. Washington, in Story of the Negro (1909), recognized him as having produced more patents than any other African-American inventor up to that time.

Will Rogers

BIRTH NAME William Penn Adair Rogers
BORN November 4, 1879
DIED August 15, 1935
DROPPED OUT High School

WILL ROGERS WAS born in the Cherokee Nation Indian Territory, near what is now Oologah, Oklahoma, and grew up on the family ranch. His parents were partly of Cherokee descent. He was one of eight children and learned to use the lasso to work with cattle on the ranch. He became so adept at using the lasso that he eventually made it to the *Guinness Book of World Records* for throwing three lassos at once.

Rogers dropped out of school in tenth grade to work as a cowboy. Five years later, he started performing rope-tricks in traveling shows, reaching South Africa, New Zealand and Australia. In 1904, he performed at the World Fairs in St Louis and New York City. After the fairs ended, he toured vaudeville circuits in America, Canada and Europe for the next decade. He started with rope tricks, but he added jokes and patter to the act. His keen observations about people, their lives and the countryside made him hugely popular as a performer. His style was simple and the audience loved his intelligent and witty remarks. He soon became more famous for his brand of humor than his rope feats.

Rogers acted in over 50 silent films and 21 talking pictures as well as Broadway productions. He was a top-box office star, voted the most popular male actor in Hollywood in 1934. He traveled the world, exchanging views with world leaders, people in the arts, and others. Although he had dropped out of school, he was always keen to learn and it was his thirst for knowledge that transformed him from a cowboy to a writer, humorist and a political commentator. He wrote six books and over 4,000 syndicated columns in addition to being a radio commentator. World leaders sought his opinion and he was a guest at the White House.

His life was cut short when he died in an air crash in 1935, at the age of 55, together with his aviator friend Wiley Post, near Point Barrow, Alaska.

It was Will Roger's quest for learning, combined with hard work that made him so successful and popular. Will Roger's wit, political writings and sayings are still relevant. His memory is kept alive by the musical *The Will Rogers Follies*, which introduces him to new audiences. The Will Rogers Institute offers funds for research in pulmonary diseases, and is a fitting memorial to the man who always thought of himself as a caring member of the human race, offering money to disaster victims and raising money for the Red Cross and Salvation Army.

Millionaire Dropouts Trivia

"I have watched all the dropouts who made their own rules" is a line in Ozzy Osbourne's song, "Crazy Train." Ozzy is a high school dropout, as is his daughter.

Andrew Lloyd Webber

BIRTH NAME Andrew Lloyd Webber
BORN March 22, 1948
DROPPED OUT Oxford University

ANDREW LLOYD WEBBER was born in London into a musically inclined family. His father, William, was a composer and scholar of music at the Royal College of Music in London; and his mother, Jean, was a piano teacher. Andrew was fascinated with ancient musical instruments and played several instruments as a child, always preferring to play to his own compositions rather than those by other composers.

Andrew's aunt took him to his first musical on stage. From then on he was fascinated with musical theatre and began composing in earnest for plays in his school. He won a scholarship to study music at Magdalen College at Oxford University in 1964, but dropped out a year later to compose musicals with lyricist Tim Rice.

After a few unsuccessful pop songs and one musical, Webber and Rice had a success on their hands in 1968 with *Joseph and the Amazing Technicolor Dreamcoat*, a biblical-themed show with a rock and roll influence. The show was a hit in England as well as the U.S. In 1971, the two produced *Jesus Christ Superstar*, which was again a big hit. Webber wrote *Jeeves* with a new partner, Alan Ayckbourn; but the musical was not a success.

Webber again teamed with Rice for *Evita*, a musical based on the life of Eva Peron, wife of the Argentine dictator. The musical opened in 1978 in London and was a huge success. It was made into a movie, starring Madonna, by Alan Parker in 1996.

Webber wrote, *Cats* based on T.S. Eliot's poems in *Old Possum's Book of Practical Cats*, in 1981. The musical went on to become his most successful production. It was a hit for its simple plot, its backdrop of interesting costumes and junkyard set. *Cats* set the record for the longest running show in London and New York, where it closed after 7,485 performances, on September 10, 2000.

In 1984 Webber wrote a musical based on trains, *Starlight Express*. His next big hit came with *The Phantom of the Opera*, in 1986, which he wrote with Charles Hart and Richard Stilgoe. Several of Webber's later musicals, such as *Aspects of Love*, in 1989, *Sunset Boulevard*, in 1993, and *Whistle Down the Wind*, in 1997, were not as successful. Recent works include *Bombay Dreams*, in 2002, with Indian composer A.R. Rehman, and *The Woman in White*, in 2004.

Webber married Sarah Hugill in 1972 and they had two children, Imogen and Nicholas. After divorcing her in 1983, Webber married Sarah Brightman in 1984, with that marriage ending in divorce in 1991. The same year he married his third wife, Madeleine Gurdon, and they have three children, Alastair, William and Isabella.

Webber has won several awards over the years including seven Tony Awards, three Grammys, six Olivier Awards, a Golden Globe, an International Emmy and an Oscar. He was also awarded the Praemium Imperiale by the Japanese Art Association and the Richard Rodgers Award for Excellence in Musical Theatre. For his contribution to British music and theatre, Webber was knighted in 1992 and became an honorary life peer of the United Kingdom in 1997.

The most successful composer of modern times, Andrew Lloyd Webber broke the mold by being innovative, blending rock and roll, classical and operatic styles to create enchanting stage musicals. He is a true genius and master of his work, constantly blending different styles to make ever more innovative and grand productions.

Adolph Zukor

BIRTH NAME Adolph Zukor
BORN January 7, 1873
DIED June 10, 1976
DROPPED OUT High School

Studio mogul Adolph Zukor, who served as the president of Paramount Pictures until 1936, lived a rags-to-riches story worthy of a Hollywood movie. He revolutionized the movie industry by bringing film production, distribution and exhibition under one company.

Zukor was born in 1873, in Ricse, Hungary, which was then a part of the Austro-Hungarian Empire. His family had to struggle to make ends meet. He came to the U.S. when he was barely 16 and worked as a sweeper in a New York fur shop for a few years before he started his own fur shop in Chicago. In 1903, he purchased an amusement arcade. He then partnered up with dropout Marcus Loew and bought a chain of arcades, eventually becoming the treasurer of Marcus Loew's chain of movie theaters.

Zukor was innovative and a man of great vision. He saw a huge potential in the movie business and found a new strategy to attract crowds to theaters. He noticed that most Americans were reluctant to go to movie theaters. Zukor wanted to create a comfortable, magical and complete theatrical experience for moviegoers. His idea was to screen longer and more dramatic films. He started with the distribution of a four-reel European film, *Queen Elizabeth*. This proved to be a good beginning and he soon made enough profit to start the Famous Players Production Company. His company became known for bringing motion picture adaptations of popular Broadway shows to theaters. The company signed the famous actress Mary Pickford for its promotions and she remained associated with the company for years.

Entrepreneur, Adolph Zukor

In 1916, Zukor merged his company with Jess L. Lasky Feature Play Company to form the Famous Players–Lasky Corporation Five years later, he became its president. Paramount Distributions was a small company then. Zukor purchased it and started buying movie theaters under the new name Paramount Pictures. In the years to come, Paramount Pictures became the biggest studio in Hollywood, with its strategy of integrating movie making and distribution.

Although Adolph Zukor was not actually involved with filmmaking, he managed the company's financial affairs from New York and the company did well till the 1930s, when it got into some financial problems. At that point, some people wanted Zukor out, but he stayed on. In 1935, Barney Balaban became Paramount's president. Zukor went on to become the company's chairman and remained so till 1976, when he died at the ripe age of 103.

Zukor's autobiography, *The Public is Never Wrong*, was published in 1953. He was successful because he understood what people wanted and also was a shrewd, hard-working and ambitious businessman. He was not born wealthy, but he created wealth with his great ideas and extraordinary vision.

Millionaire Dropouts Trivia

Madame C.J. Walker, the first African-American millionaire, was a dropout.

$ Millionaire Dropouts Trivia $

America's richest high school dropout, J.R. Simplot, is worth $4.7 billion.

Filmmakers

Filmmakers

Filmmakers

Filmmakers

Filmmakers

Filmmakers

Filmmakers

Filmmakers

Filmmakers

James Cameron

BIRTH NAME James Francis Cameron
BORN August 16, 1954
DROPPED OUT Fullerton College

JAMES CAMERON WAS born in Kapuskasing, Ontario. His father, Philip, was an electrical engineer and his mother, Shirley, was an artist. As a child James showed his propensity for leadership among his friends, instigating the building of go-carts, rockets and catapults. Encouraged by his mother, he painted, exhibiting his work at a local gallery. One of his earliest inspirations was the film, *2001: A Space Odyssey*. He began to experiment with filmmaking and photographed the model space ships he built.

The family moved to Fullerton, California, in 1971. Cameron enrolled in Fullerton College, majoring in physics and later in English, eventually dropping out of college, as he was unable to decide if he should focus on art or science. *Star Wars* rekindled his fascination with film production and he decided to study on his own terms, using the resources of the library of the University of Southern California to study special effects technology, optical printing and projection techniques.

Cameron's first job was at the Roger Corman Studios as a miniature model maker. He progressed to become an art director for the sci-fi movie *Battle Beyond the Stars* and also worked on *Escape from New York*. His big break came in 1981 when he was chosen by Italian producer Ovidio G. Assonitis to make *Piranha Part Two: The Spawning*. Assonitis had selected Cameron to save money and to have full control over the movie, but Cameron wanted to have creative license and the two fought constantly. The movie was underfinanced and had an Italian crew who knew no English; it ended up being a disaster.

Cameron was constantly under stress because the low quality of his work. He had a nightmare about an invisible robot hit man sent from the future to kill him—the birth of the *Terminator* series. As he wanted to direct the film himself, Cameron was rejected by the major studios. He eventually made a deal with producer Gale Anne Hurd, selling her the movie rights for one dollar. It was his unending enthusiasm and passion that convinced Arnold Schwarzenegger to star in the film. *The Terminator* was a huge success and paved Cameron's way in Hollywood, establishing his reputation as a screenwriter and director.

Cameron wrote the screenplays of *Rambo: First Blood Part 2* and *Aliens* while waiting for *The Terminator* to be financed. With the film's success, he was asked to direct *Aliens*, which won Oscars for best visual effects and best sound effects. In the following years Cameron made action films including *The Abyss, Point Break, Terminator 2: Judgment Day* and *True Lies*.

Cameron surprised everyone by selecting a love story set on the doomed ocean liner *Titanic* as his next film. After a grueling schedule that was millions of dollars over budget, the movie created history by breaking box office records the world over. It became the top grossing film of all time. Starring Leonardo DiCaprio and Kate Winslet, the movie won eleven Academy Awards, including best director and best picture.

Cameron's single-minded focus on films has led to upheavals in his private life. He has been married five times, to Sharon Williams, producer Gale Anne Hurd, director Katherine Bigelow, *Terminator* star Linda Hamilton and Suzy Amis.

James Cameron has succeeded in Hollywood on his own terms, creating his art with a passion few possess and at a high personal cost. He never learned to accept defeat, always finding a way to succeed. He believes in creating his own destiny, never taking 'no' for an answer.

Peter Jackson

BIRTH NAME Peter Jackson
BORN October 31, 1961
DROPPED OUT High School

PETER JACKSON WAS born in Wellington and grew up in the neighboring town of Pukerua Bay in New Zealand. As an only child, he developed a vivid imagination and gave free rein to it when his parents received an 8 mm camera as a gift in 1969. Mastering camera techniques, Peter began making movies with it, dropping out of high school and getting a job at the local newspaper. Born on Halloween, he became fascinated with horror movies after seeing films such as *Evil Dead* and *Dawn of the Dead*.

Working as a cinematographer for various TV shows in New Zealand from the age of seventeen, Jackson made his directorial debut with *Roast of the Day*, in 1983, a ten-minute short that was later expanded to a feature-length movie, *Bad Taste*. The movie became a cult classic and set the tone for Jackson's style of cinema, full of blood, guts and gore. His next film was *Meet the Feebles*, a story about a group of puppets and their television show, which again was a feast of twisted humor, graphic violence and Jackson's trademark blood and guts scenes.

Jackson's next film, *Brain Dead*, re-titled *Dead Alive* for U.S. audiences, was named by the New York *Daily News* as "the goriest fright film of all time." The movie surpassed his earlier movies, showing an unending stream of blood and severed limbs. With each of his first three films, he earned appreciation among cultists and became firmly entrenched as the king of gore.

In 1994, Jackson made *Heavenly Creatures*, starring Kate Winslet, a true story about two schoolgirls who murdered one's mother. The movie was well received and won several honors, including the Silver Lion at the Venice Film Festival. His next few movies, *The Frighteners*, starring Michael J. Fox, *Forgotten Silver*, a black and white film

Filmmaker, Peter Jackson

narrated by Sam Neill and *Jack Brown, Genius*, based on the life of historically neglected New Zealand filmmaker Colin McKenzie, were all commercially and critically disappointing.

Jackson started his most ambitious plan in 1998, adapting J.R.R. Tolkien's famous trilogy *Lord of the Rings*, for which he selected a large and talented cast. The first film, *Lord of the Rings: The Fellowship of the Ring*, was a huge success; it received thirteen Oscar nominations and won for best cinematography, best visual effects, best makeup and best score. The second movie, *The Lord of the Rings: The Two Towers*, was an even bigger commercial success and received six Oscar nominations, winning for best sound editing and best visual effects. The third movie, *The Lord of the Rings: The Return of the King*, again opened to rave reviews and huge commercial success and went on to win all eleven Oscars it had been nominated for, tying with *Ben-Hur* and *Titanic* for the most Oscars won by a single film.

Instead of moving to Hollywood, Jackson makes his movies in his native New Zealand, which has led to great deal of business in Miramar to support his film production. Taking advantage of the time difference between New Zealand and the U.S., Jackson provides digital special effects to several Hollywood films via telecommunication and satellite links.

Peter Jackson is fiercely independent, famously offbeat and a perfectionist. He is one of the few horror movie directors to have bridged the gap to mainstream cinema and is respected for his intense dedication on *Lord of the Rings*. He has a large cult following for his gory style of cinema.

Michael Moore

BIRTH NAME Michael Moore
BORN April 23, 1954
DROPPED OUT University of Michigan–Flint

MICHAEL MOORE WAS born in Davison, Michigan. Both his father and grandfather worked at the local General Motors plant and lost their jobs when GM closed the factory. These issues played an important part in shaping Moore's passion for revealing corporate injustice and greed.

In high school, Moore created a slide show that exposed environmentally unfriendly businesses, setting the tone for future projects. He became one of the youngest people elected to public office when he won a seat on the Flint School Board in 1972, when he was 18. Enrolling at the University of Michigan–Flint, Moore dropped out soon after to focus on activism and started working at a local newspaper, *The Flint Voice*. Soon becoming the editor, he expanded the paper to cover the entire Midwest. He then joined *Mother Jones* magazine as editor, but his confrontational style led to his being fired in less than a year.

Moore worked briefly for a Ralph Nader organization and then decided to make a film about his hometown, Flint, and the impact of the closure of General Motors automobile plants on the local economy. The result, *Roger & Me* was one of the most commercially successful documentary films ever made and received honors at several film festivals. He followed up with *Pets or Meat: The Return to Flint*, a half-hour television film that was a continuation of *Roger & Me*.

Moore's first fictional film was *Canadian Bacon*, a black comedy starring John Candy, who died soon after. Moore then produced a satiric news and commentary show called *TV Nation*, a summer replacement show that attracted a small fan base but lasted only two

Filmmaker, Michael Moore

seasons. Moore produced another television show, *The Awful Truth*, a mix of comedy and political commentary. It aired in 1999 and 2000.

Moore published a book, *Downsize This!: Random Threats From an Unarmed American*, which became a bestseller. While he traveled across the U.S. promoting the book, Moore made a documentary titled, *The Big One*, capturing economic inequality in the country. His next book, *Stupid White Men*, was published in early 2002 and was a major bestseller. The book openly criticized George W. Bush.

Increasingly in the media spotlight for his controversial opinions, Moore became widely known. His next film, *Bowling for Columbine*, delved into the country's fascination with guns and violence. It was featured at the Cannes Film Festival, where it received the Jury Award. The film also won the 2002 Oscar for best documentary

Moore's most famous and controversial film was *Fahrenheit 9/11*, a hard-hitting look at the Bush administration's ties to Osama bin Laden's family and the Bush family's ulterior motives for going to war. The film won the Palm D'Or at the Cannes Film Festival in 2004 and was both a commercial and critical success.

Michael Moore uses his trademark wit and caustic humor to report on injustice and malfeasance. As a fearless investigator of and commentator on political and economic attitudes in America, he has carved out a place for himself as an iconoclast, gadfly and defender of the common man.

Millionaire Dropouts Trivia

One of the top-grossing films of 2005, War of the Worlds, was written by a dropout (H.G. Wells), was directed by a dropout (Steven Spielberg) and starred a dropout (Tom Cruise).

Millionaire Dropouts Trivia

America's richest college dropout is Bill Gates.

Your Personal Biography

Your Personal Biography

Your Personal Biography

Your Personal Biography

Your Personal Biography

Your Personal Biography

Your Personal Biography

Your Personal Biography

Your Personal Biography

Millionaire Dropouts

Your Name _____

BIRTH NAME _____
BORN _____
DROPPED OUT _____

_____
_____
_____
_____
_____
_____
_____
_____
_____
_____
_____
_____
_____

FAME_____ NAME_____

Appendix

HERE IS A list of some prominent dropouts in many fields. They did not all achieve great wealth; many achieved greatness in other ways. All of them have fascinating life stories, though.

I've included just a few words about each person to remind you of why you might have heard of them.

Name	Reminder	Dropped Out
	The World of Business	
	Billionaires	
Roman Abramovich	Oil	College
Sheldon Adelson	Casinos, hotels	College
Paul Allen	Microsoft	College
Herbert Allen Jr.	Investment banker	High school
Dhirubhai Ambani	Reliance Group—textiles	High school
Micky Arison	Carnival Cruise Line	High school
Steven Ballmer	Microsoft	College
Bill Bartman	Wall Street—filed bankruptcy twice	High school
Richard Branson	Virgin Enterprises	High school
James Cayne	Bear Stearns	College
Jim Clark	Netscape	High school
Jack Cooke	Broadcasting	High school
Constantino De Oliveira Jr.	Airline entrepreneur	College
Michael Dell	Dell Computers	College
Richard Desmond	British newspaper publisher	High school
Barry Diller	Television executive	College
Charles Dolan	Cablevision Systems	College
Larry Ellison	Oracle	College
David Filo	Yahoo!	College
Thomas Flatley	Real estate	College
Sidney Frank	Grey Goose vodka	College
Yoshitaka Fukuda	Credit banking	High school
Bill Gates	Microsoft	College
David Geffen	Dreamworks SKG	College
Alan Gerry	Cablevision	High school
Lim Goh Tong	Gaming	High school
Thomas Haffa	Media	High school
Kenneth Hendricks	Building supplies	High school
Stanley Ho	Gaming	College
H. Wayne Huizenga	Blockbuster Video, team owner	College
H.L. Hunt	Oil industrialist	Elementary school

www.MillionaireDropouts.com

Appendix

Name	Reminder	Dropped Out
\multicolumn{3}{c}{The World of Business *(continued)*}		
\multicolumn{3}{c}{*Billionaires (continued)*}		
Carl Icahn	Corporate raider	College
James Jannard	Oakley sunglasses	College
Steve Jobs	Apple Computer	College
Li Ka-shing	Investor	High school
Kirk Kerkorian	Investor	High school
Ray Kroc	McDonald's	High school
Ralph Lauren	Polo	College
Joe Lewis	Investor	High school
Richard Li	Telecom	College
Carl Lindner Jr.	American Financial Group	High school
Robert Maxwell	Publisher	High school
William Morean	Jabil Circuit	College
David H. Murdock	CEO Dole Foods	High school
Donald Newhouse	Publisher	College
Amancio Ortega	Apparel	High school
Gregorio Perez	Oil and gas	High school
John D. Rockefeller	Standard Oil	High school
Winthrop Rockefeller	Banking	College
Kjell Inge Rokke	Industrialist	High school
Phillip Ruffin	Casino, real estate	College
Edmond Safra	Banking	High school
Yasumitsu Shigeta	Telecom	College
J.R. Simplot	French fries	High school
Daniel Snyder	Sports team owner	College
Sheldon Solow	Real estate	College
Steven Spielberg	*E.T., Indiana Jones;* Oscar winner	College
A. Alfred Taubman	Real estate	College
Jack Taylor	Enterprise Rent-A-Car	College
Ted Turner	Media mogul	College
Donald John Tyson	Tyson Foods	College
Albert Ueltschi	Flight safety training school	College
Theodore Waitt	Gateway	College
Ty Warner	Ty Beanie Babies	College
Hiroshi Yamauchi	Nintendo Corporation	College
Jerry Yang	Yahoo!	College
Ahmet Zorlu	Electronics	High school
\multicolumn{3}{c}{*Millionaires*}		
John Jacob Astor	America's first millionaire	High school
Asa Candler	Coca-Cola pioneer	College
Kevin Cannon	Freight Software	College
Andrew Carnegie	Legacy	Elementary school
Charles E. Culpeper	Coca Cola bottler	High school
Thomas Gallagher	Vice-president CIBC Oppenheimer	College
Richard Grasso	New York Stock Exchange	College
Kevin Liles	Warner Music Group, Def Jam	College
Del E. Webb	Developer; Yankees owner	High school

www.MillionaireDropouts.com

Millionaire Dropouts

The World of Business (*continued*)

Company Founders

Name	Reminder	Dropped Out
Wally Amos	Famous Amos Cookies	High school
Walter Anderson	White Castle Hamburger	College
Anne Beiler	Auntie Anne's	High school
Joe Biedenharn	Coca-Cola Bottling	High school
William Boeing	Boeing Aircraft	College
Milton Bradley	Toys	College
Dov Charney	American Apparel	College
Ben Cohen	Ben & Jerry's Ice Cream	College
Harry Cohn	Columbia Pictures	High school
Sean "P. Diddy" Combs	Sean John clothing, Bad Boy Records	College
Joshua Lionel Cowen	Lionel Trains	College
Jimmy Dean	Jimmy Dean Foods	High school
Xavier Delacour	Attune LLC	High school
Walt Disney	Disney Studios	High school
Charles Dow	Dow Jones	High school
Matt Drudge	Drudge Report	High school
George Eastman	Eastman Kodak	High school
Max Factor	Max Factor cosmetics	Elementary school
Shawn Fanning	Napster	College
Henry Ford	Ford Motor Company	High school
Patrick Frawley	Papermate Pens	High school
James Gamble	Procter & Gamble	High school
Amadeo Peter Giannini	Bank of America	High school
King Gillette	Gillette razors	High school
Berry Gordy	Motown Records	High school
Florence Graham	Elizabeth Arden cosmetics	College
W.T. Grant	W.T. Grant Stores	High school
Horace Greeley	*New York Tribune*; U.S. Congress	High school
Ruth Handler	Mattel; Barbie Doll	College
Fred Harvey	Harvey House restaurants	High school
Milton Hershey	Hershey Chocolate	Elementary school
Soichiro Honda	Honda	High school
John H Johnson	Ebony, Jet magazines	College
Edward Jones	Dow Jones	College
Henry J. Kaiser	Kaiser Aluminum	High school
Edwin H. Land	Polaroid	College
Marcus Loew	MGM; Loews Theatres	High school
Mary Lyon	Mount Holyoke College	High school
John Mackey	Whole Foods	College
Frank Mars	Mars Candy	High school
Tom Monaghan	Domino's Pizza	College
Eric Morley	Miss World Pageant	High school
Christopher Morrison	PLPDigital Systems	College
David Neelman	Jet Blue	College
Mary Pickford	United Artists	High school
Joseph Pulitzer	*New York World*	High school
Bill Rosenberg	Dunkin' Donuts	High school

APPENDIX

Name	Reminder	Dropped Out
\multicolumn{3}{c}{The World of Business (continued)}		
\multicolumn{3}{c}{Company Founders (continued)}		
Harold Ross	*The New Yorker*	High school
Frederick Henry Royce	Rolls Royce	Elementary school
Rick Rubin	Def Jam Records	College
Harland Sanders	Kentucky Fried Chicken	Elementary school
Margaret Sanger	American Birth Control League	College
David Sarnoff	RCA, NBC	High school
Vidal Sassoon	Vidal Sassoon Hair Products	High school
W. Clement Stone	*Success Magazine*	Elementary school
Alan Sugar	Amstrad	High school
Dave Thomas	Wendy's	High school
Jann Wenner	*Rolling Stone*	College
George Westinghouse	Westinghouse Electric Company	College
Kemmons Wilson	Holiday Inn	High school
Steve Wozniak	Apple Computer	College
William Wrigley Jr.	Wrigley's Gum	High school
\multicolumn{3}{c}{Entrepreneurs}		
John Barfield	The Bartech Group	High school
Carl G. Fisher	Developer	Elementary school
Freddie Laker	Airline	High school
David Martin	Martin Zambito Art Gallery	High school
Frank McKinney	Builder	College
Mary-Kate Olsen	Olsen twins	College
Tim Paulson	Writer, coach	College
Stanley Perron	Real estate, Australia's ninth richest man	High school
Muriel Siebert	First woman member, NYSE	College
Dawn Steel	Columbia Pictures	College
Ryan Tewis	Real estate	College
Travis Tollestrup	Real estate	College
Charles Urban	Movie theatres	High school
Jimmie Wedell	Aviation school owner	College
Dave Woodward	Marketing guru	College
Frank Woodward	Jell-O	High school
Woody Woodward	Sold first idea at age 16	High school
Dominick Zambito	Martin Zambito Art Gallery	High school
Adolph Zukor	Paramount Pictures	High school
\multicolumn{3}{c}{Executives}		
R.J. Funkhouser	Banker	Elementary school
Wayne Inouye	Gateway Computers	College
Allen W. Jacobson	Boeing manager	High school
Harry Winston	Jeweler	High school
\multicolumn{3}{c}{The World of Technology}		
\multicolumn{3}{c}{Scientists and Engineers}		
Herbert Brown	Chemist	High school
Albert Einstein	Physicist	High school

Millionaire Dropouts

Name	Reminder	Dropped Out
\multicolumn{3}{c}{The World of Technology *(continued)*}		

The World of Technology *(continued)*

Scientists and Engineers *(continued)*

Name	Reminder	Dropped Out
Michael Faraday	Physicist	High school
Oliver Heaviside	Applied mathematician	High school
Jaron Lanier	Computer scientist; virtual reality pioneer	High school
Arthur Ernest Morgan	Flood control engineer	High school
Valentina Tereshkova	Cosmonaut, first woman in space	High school
Anton van Leeuwenhok	Microscope maker; discovered bacteria	High school
Frank Lloyd Wright	Architect	College

Inventors

Name	Reminder	Dropped Out
Ole Kirk Christian	Legos	Elementary school
James B. Eads	Steel-arch bridge	High school
Thomas Edison	Over 2,000 patents	Elementary school
Oliver Evans	Steam engine	High school
Philo T. Farnsworth	Television	College
Chester Greenwood	Earmuffs	Elementary school
Frederick Jones	Refrigerated truck	High school
Dean Kamen	Segway	College
Gordon Langford	Flexpoint sensor	College
William Lear	Learjet	High school
Adolph Levis	Slim Jim	High school
Guglielmo Marconi	Wireless telegraphy (radio)	Elementary school
Hiram Maxim	Machine-gun	High school
Elijah McCoy	Automatic lubricator; ironing board	High school
Florence Melton	Foam slippers	High school
Garrett Morgan	Traffic signal; gas mask; protective gear	High school
Earl Muntz	Car stereo tape deck; affordable TV set	High school
James Naismith	Basketball	High school
Isaac Merrit Singer	Practical sewing machine	Elementary school
Nikola Tesla	Radio	High school
C.J. Walker	Hair products	Elementary school
Orville Wright	Airplane	High school
Wilbur Wright	Airplane	High school

The Media

Publishers

Name	Reminder	Dropped Out
Felix Dennis	*Maxim Magazine*	High school
Jimmy Lai	Hong Kong media tycoon	Elementary school
Adolph Ochs	*New York Times*	High school
Henry Parks	Australian newspaper publisher, politician	High school
Lyle Stuart	Publisher of controversial books	High school

Editors

Name	Reminder	Dropped Out
Mortimer Adler	*Encyclopedia Britannica*	High school
Walter Anderson	*Parade*	High school
Karl Hess	*Newsweek*	High school
Diana Vreeland	Fashion magazines	High school

Appendix

Name	Reminder	Dropped Out
\multicolumn{3}{c}{The Media (continued)}		

The Media (continued)

Journalists

Name	Reminder	Dropped Out
Tucker Carlson	*Crossfire*	College
John Chancellor	*NBC Nightly News*	High school
Walter Cronkite	CBS News	College
Pete Hamill	*New York Post*	High school
Peter Jennings	*ABC World News Tonight*	High school
Matt Lauer	*Today Show*	College
Andrea Thompson	*CNN Headline News*	High school
Nina Totenberg	National Public Radio	College

Television Personalities

Name	Reminder	Dropped Out
Simon Cowell	*American Idol* judge, music producer	High school
Bill Cullen	Game show host	High school
Carson Daly	Talk show host	College
Jenny Jones	Talk show host	High school
Lisa Ling	Talk show host	College
Frank Nicotero	Game show host	College
Jack Paar	Talk show host	High school
Lawrence Welk	TV bandleader	High school

Radio Personalities

Name	Reminder	Dropped Out
Art Bell	Hosts paranormal-themed shows	High school
Don Imus	*Imus in the Morning*	High school
Wolfman Jack	Top 40 rock and roll pioneer	High school
Rush Limbaugh	Talk show host	College
Ron Reagan Jr.	Political commentator	College

Society at Large

Academics

Name	Reminder	Dropped Out
Daniel Gilbert	Harvard psychology professor	High school
Hubert Bancroft	Historian	High school
Walter L. Smith	President, Florida A&M University	High school

Social Activists

Name	Reminder	Dropped Out
Brooke Astor	Philanthropist	High school
Erin Brockovich	Environmental activist	High school
Margaret Brown	Philanthropist, Titanic survivor	High school
Cesar Chavez	Farmworker rights activist	High school
Diana, Princess of Wales	Philanthropist	High school
Samuel Gompers	Labor rights activist	Elementary school
John Llewellyn	Labor rights activist	High school
Florence Nightingale	Nursing pioneer	High school
Rosa Parks	Civil rights activist	High school
Oral Roberts	Evangelist	High school
Malcolm X	Civil rights activist	High school

Popular Culture Notables

Name	Reminder	Dropped Out
Daniel Boone	Frontiersman	High school
Gisele Bündchen	Model	High school

Millionaire Dropouts

Name	Reminder	Dropped Out
\multicolumn{3}{c}{Society at Large *(continued)*}		
\multicolumn{3}{c}{*Popular Culture Notables (continued)*}		
Brooke Burke	Model; TV host	College
Jackie Cochran	Aviation pioneer	Elementary school
William Cody	*Buffalo Bill's Wild West Show*	Elementary school
Christopher Columbus	Explorer	High school
James Cook	Explorer	High school
Cindy Crawford	Model	College
Davy Crockett	Frontiersman, Congressman	High school
Heidi Dinan	Mrs. America 2004	College
Elizabeth Jagger	Model	High school
Evel Knievel	Daredevil	High school
Henrietta Leaver	Model; Miss America 1935	High school
Audrey Marnay	Model	High school
Jenny McCarthy	Model, actress, MTV host	College
Heather Mills	Model; anti-land mine activist	High school
Annie Oakley	Sharpshooter; entertainer	High school
Philippe Petit	High wire performer	High school
Sam Phillips	Rock and roll pioneer	High school
Paulina Porizkova	Model	High school
Eddie Rickenbacker	World War I flying ace	High school
Will Rogers	Humorist	High school
Rebecca Romijn-Stamos	Model	College
Robert F. Scott	Explorer	High school
Molly Sims	Model	College
Henry Stanley	Explorer	High school
\multicolumn{3}{c}{*Politicians and Statesmen*}		
Cruz Bustamante	California lieutenant governor	College
Ben Nighthorse Cambell	U.S. senator	High school
Richard Carmona	U.S. surgeon general	High school
Grover Cleveland	U.S. president	High school
James Farley	Postmaster general under FDR	Elementary school
Millard Fillmore	U.S. president	Elementary school
James Florio	New Jersey governor 1990–1994	High school
Benjamin Franklin	Printer, inventor, statesman	High school
Mohandes Gandhi	Indian independence leader	High school
Barry Goldwater	U.S. senator	College
Roy Greensmith	Sheriff of Nottingham, U.K., 1995–1996	High school
William Henry Harrison	U.S. president	High school
Arthur Henderson	Co-founder of Britain's Labor Party	High school
Patrick Henry	Virginia's first governor	Elementary school
Andrew Jackson	U.S. president	High school
Andrew Johnson	U.S. president	High school
John Paul Jones	Naval commander	High school
Leon Jouhaux	French labor leader	High school
Bernard Kerik	New York police commissioner	High school
Abraham Lincoln	U.S. president	Elementary school

Appendix

Name	Reminder	Dropped Out
\multicolumn{3}{c}{Society at Large *(continued)*}		
\multicolumn{3}{c}{Politicians and Statesmen *(continued)*}		
John Major	British prime minister 1990–1997	High school
Thomas Maltby	Australian political leader	High school
Mike Mansfield	U.S. senator	High school
William McKinley	U.S. president	College
Melina Mercouri	Greek politician; actress	High school
Ruth Ann Minner	Delaware governor 2001–2005	High school
Joseph Moakley	U.S. congressman	High school
James Monroe	U.S. president	College
Walter Nash	New Zealand prime minister, 1957–1960	High school
Evita Peron	Argentinian political leader	High school
Charles Rangel	U.S. congressman	High school
James E. Rogan	U.S. congressman	High school
Karl Rove	White House senior advisor	College
Arnold Schwarzenegger	Governor of California	High school
Alfred Smith	New York governor, 1928 presidential nominee	Elementary school
Zachary Taylor	U.S. president	High school
Harry Truman	U.S. president	College
Martin Van Buren	U.S. president	High school
Antonio Villaraigosa	Mayor of Los Angeles	High school
George Washington	U.S. president	High school
\multicolumn{3}{c}{The Fine Arts}		
\multicolumn{3}{c}{Writers}		
Hans Christian Andersen	Children's stories	High school
Jane Austen	*Pride and Prejudice*	Elementary school
John Bartlett	*Bartlett's Familiar Quotations*	High school
Barbara Taylor Bradford	Romance novels	High school
Rick Bragg	*Ava's Man*	College
Hall Caines	*The Christian*	Elementary school
Albert Camus	*The Plague*	High school
Truman Capote	*Breakfast at Tiffany's*	High school
Raymond Chandler	Noir detective novels	College
G. K. Chesterton	*The Man Who Was Thursday*	College
Agatha Christie	*Death on the Nile*	Elementary school
Samuel L. Clemens	*Tom Sawyer*	Elementary school
Jackie Collins	*Hollywood Husbands*	High school
Joseph Conrad	*Heart of Darkness*	High school
Lloyd Dennis	*His Way Works*	High school
Charles Dickens	*A Christmas Carol*	Elementary school
James Dickey	*Deliverance*	High school
James Ellroy	*L.A. Confidential*	High school
Howard Fast	*Spartacus*	High school
William Faulkner	*The Sound and the Fury*	High school
F Scott Fitzgerald	*The Great Gatsby*	College
Shelby Foote	*The Civil War*	College
Henry George	*Progress and Poverty*	Elementary school

Millionaire Dropouts

Name	Reminder	Dropped Out
\multicolumn{3}{c}{The Fine Arts (continued)}		

The Fine Arts (continued)

Writers (continued)

Name	Reminder	Dropped Out
Alex Haley	Roots	High school
Eric Hoffer	The True Believer	High school
Louis L'Amour	Westerns	High school
Fran Lebowitz	Metropolitan Life	High school
Doris Lessing	Children of Violence	High school
Jack London	Call of the Wild	High school
Richard Marcinko	Rogue Warrior	High school
Harry Martinson	Wild Bouquet	High school
Moa Martinson	My Mother Gets Married	High school
Oseola McCarty	Riches of Oseola McCarty	Elementary school
Herman Melville	Moby-Dick	High school
Dave Pelzer	The Privilege of Youth	High school
Edgar Allen Poe	Horror stories, poetry	College
Harold Robbins	The Carpetbaggers	High school
Nora Roberts	Naked in Death	High school
J.D. Salinger	The Catcher In the Rye	College
Carl Sandburg	Abraham Lincoln	High school
José Saramago	Baltasar and Blimunda	High school
John Steinbeck	The Grapes of Wrath	High school
Leo Tolstoy	War and Peace	College
H.G. Wells	War of the Worlds	High school
Richard Wright	Native Son	High school

Poets

Name	Reminder	Dropped Out
Maya Angelou	The Heart of a Woman	College
William Blake	Songs of Innocence	High school
Joseph Brodsky	A Part of Speech	High school
John Clare	The Rural Muse	High school
Robert Frost	In the Clearing	Elementary school
Langston Hughes	Shakespeare in Harlem	College
Gwendolyn MacEwen	The Fire-Eaters	High school
Rod McKuen	Listen to the Warm	Elementary school
Banjo Paterson	Australian bush poet, "Waltzing Matilda"	High school
Alexander Pope	The Rape of the Lock	High school
Patti Smith	Auguries of Innocence	College
Ron Whitehead	I Will Not Bow Down	High school
Walt Whitman	Leaves of Grass	Elementary school

Composers and Songwriters

Name	Reminder	Dropped Out
Peter Allen	"I Go To Rio"	High school
Gene Autry	"Here Comes Santa Claus"	High school
Irving Berlin	"White Christmas"	High school
Jacques Brel	Belgian actor, author, composer, poet	High school
Sammy Cahn	"High Hopes"	High school
Jim Dale	"Georgy Girl"	High school
Thomas Dolby	"She Blinded Me with Science"	High school
Duke Ellington	"Black, Brown and Beige"	High school

Appendix

Name	Reminder	Dropped Out
\multicolumn{3}{c}{*The Fine Arts (continued)*}		

The Fine Arts (continued)

Composers and Songwriters (continued)

Name	Reminder	Dropped Out
George Gershwin	*Rhapsody in Blue*	High school
Burton Lane	"How are Things in Glocca Morra?"	High school
Oscar Levant	Broadway and Hollywood composer	High school
John Philip Sousa	"Stars and Stripes Forever"	Elementary school
Andrew Lloyd Webber	*The Phantom of the Opera, Evita, Cats*	College
John Zorn	Avant-garde composer	College

Playwrights and Screen Writers

Name	Reminder	Dropped Out
Edward Albee	*Who's Afraid of Virginia Woolf?*	College
Sean O'Casey	*The Plough and the Stars*	Elementary school
John Fusco	*Hidalgo*	High school
Garson Kanin	*Born Yesterday*	High achool
Elaine May	*A New Leaf*	High achool
Tim Rice	Lyricist, *Jesus Christ, Superstar; The Lion King*	College
William Saroyan	*The Time of Your Life*	High achool
William Shakespeare	*Romeo and Juliet*	High school
George Bernard Shaw	*Pygmalion*	High school
Tennessee Williams	*Cat on a Hot Tin Roof*	College
August Wilson	*Ma Rainey's Black Bottom*	High school

Artists

Name	Reminder	Dropped Out
Edwin Apps	*Fishers of Men*	High school
James Flagg	Illustrator; "I Want You for the U.S. Army" poster	High school
Claude Monet	*Water Lilies*	Elementary school
LeRoy Neiman	Sports and jazz portraits	High school
Yoko Ono	Performance art, conceptual art	College
Lesser Ury	*City Lights*	High school
Vincent Van Gogh	*Starry Night*	High school

Photographers and Sculptors

Name	Reminder	Dropped Out
Ansel Adams	Wilderness photographer	High school
Richard Avedon	Fashion and portrait photographer	High school
Helmut Newton	Fashion and figure photographer	High school
Gordon Parks	*Life* magazine photographer; polymath	High school
Edward Leedskalnin	Sculptor, *Coral Castle* in Homestead, Florida	Elementary school

Fashion Designers

Name	Reminder	Dropped Out
Miguel Adrover	Avant-garde designer	High school
Liz Claiborne	Liz Claiborne, Inc.	High school
Tom Ford	Gucci	College
Alexander McQueen	Givenchy	High school
Gloria Vanderbilt	Designer jeans	High school

Filmmakers

Name	Reminder	Dropped Out
Woody Allen	*Annie Hall*	College
Paul Anderson	*Boogie Nights*	High school
Peter Bogdanovich	*Mask*	High school
John Boorman	*The Tailor of Panama*	High school

Millionaire Dropouts

Name	Reminder	Dropped Out
\multicolumn{3}{c}{*The Fine Arts (continued)*}		
\multicolumn{3}{c}{*Filmmakers (continued)*}		
Stan Brakhage	Work in Progress	College
James Cameron	Titanic	College
Robert Evans	Chinatown	High school
Samuel Fuller	The Day of Reckoning	High school
Lew Grade	The Muppet Movie	High school
D.W. Griffith	Birth of a Nation	High school
William Hanna	Animator, Hanna–Barbera Productions	College
John Huston	The Maltese Falcon	High school
Peter Jackson	Lord of the Rings	High school
Stanley Kubrick	2001: A Space Odyssey	High school
David Lean	Dr. Zhivago	High school
Joseph Levine	The Graduate	High school
Michael Moore	Fahrenheit 9/11	High school
Jon Peters	The Color Purple	Elementary school
David Puttman	Chariots of Fire	High school
Guy Ritchie	Swept Away	High school
Kevin Smith	Clerks	College
Robert Stigwood	Saturday Night Fever	High school
Quentin Tarantino	Pulp Fiction	High school
François Truffaut	The 400 Blows	High school
John Woo	Broken Arrow	High school

The Performing Arts

Dancers

Name	Reminder	Dropped Out
Josephine Baker	U.S. expatriate star in Europe	High school
Isadora Duncan	Mother of modern dance	Elementary school
Lola Falana	U.S. dancer, actress	High school
Bill "Bojangles" Robinson	U.S. tap dancer	Elementary school

Musicians and Singers

Name	Reminder	Dropped Out
Bryan Adams	Canadian singer–songwriter	High school
Christina Aguilera	U.S. singer–songwriter	High school
Rick Allen	Def Leppard drummer	High school
Joan Armatrading	U.K. singer–songwriter	High school
Louis Armstrong	Jazz trumpeter, singer	High school
Eddy Arnold	Country music singer	High school
Chet Atkins	Country music guitarist	High school
Pearl Bailey	U.S. singer	High school
Shirley Bassey	Welsh singer	High school
Beck	U.S. musician	High school
André Benjamin	Rapper André 3000 of OutKast	High school
Chuck Berry	Rock pioneer; singer–composer	High school
Mary J. Blige	U.S. singer–songwriter	High school
Clint Black	Country singer–songwriter	High school
Norman Blake	U.S. songwriter–musician	High school
Michael Bolton	U.S. singer–songwriter	High school
Sonny Bono	U.S. singer, producer, politician	High school

Appendix

Name	Reminder	Dropped Out
\multicolumn{3}{c}{The Performing Arts (continued)}		
\multicolumn{3}{c}{Musicians and Singers (continued)}		
David Bowie	U.K. singer, musician, writer	High school
Billy Bragg	U.K. folk and protest musician	High school
Gary Brooker	Procol Harum pianist, singer–songwriter	High school
Pete Burns	U.K. singer–songwriter	Elementary school
David Byrne	Talking Heads songwriter	College
Glen Campbell	Country singer	High school
Viki Carr	U.S. singer	High school
Ray Charles	U.S. pianist–singer	High school
Cher	U.S. singer, actress	High school
Eric Clapton	U.K. guitarist, composer, singer	High school
Kurt Cobain	Nirvana singer–songwriter	High school
Eddie Cochran	U.S. rockabilly musician	High school
Joe Cocker	U.K. rock and blues musician	High school
Phil Collins	Genesis lead singer, drummer	High school
Russ Conway	U.K. pianist	High school
Perry Como	U.S. crooner	High school
Elvis Costello	U.K. singer–songwriter	High school
Roger Daltry	Lead singer, The Who	High school
Vic Damone	U.S. singer	High school
Sammy Davis Jr.	U.S. singer, dancer, comedian, actor	Elementary school
Neil Diamond	U.S. singer	College
Bo Diddley	U.S. singer–songwriter	High school
Celine Dion	Canadian pop singer	High school
Steve Earle	Country singer–songwriter	High school
Eminem	Rap artist	High school
Adam Faith	U.K. singer, actor	High school
Perry Farrell	U.S. alternative rock musician	College
José Feliciano	Puerto Rican singer	High school
Ella Fitzgerald	U.S. jazz singer	High school
Peter Frampton	U.K. rock musician	High school
Aretha Franklin	U.S. singer	High school
Jerry Garcia	Grateful Dead guitarist, lead singer	High school
Mary Gauthier	U.S. folksinger–songwriter	High school
Marvin Gaye	U.S. singer–songwriter, producer	High school
Boy George	Culture Club singer–songwriter	High school
Andy Gibb	U.K.–Australian singer	Elementary school
Barry Gibb	U.K. singer–songwriter, the Bee Gees	High school
Maurice Gibb	U.K. musician, the Bee Gees	High school
Robin Gibb	U.K. singer, the Bee Gees	High school
Dizzy Gillespie	Jazz trumpeter	High school
Benny Goodman	U.S. clarinetist, swing bandleader	High school
Graham Gouldman	U.K. songwriter, bass player	High school
Josh Groban	U.S. singer–songwriter	College
Dave Grohl	Nirvana, Foo Fighters drummer	High school
Arlo Guthrie	U.S. folksinger–songwriter	College
Woody Guthrie	U.S. folksinger–songwriter	High school
Merle Haggard	U.S. singer–songwriter	High school

Millionaire Dropouts

The Performing Arts (*continued*)

Musicians and Singers (*continued*)

Name	Reminder	Dropped Out
Bill Haley	U.S. rock and roll pioneer	High school
Jet Harris	Bass guitarist, The Shadows	High school
George Harrison	Beatles singer–songwriter	High school
Beth Hart	U.S. singer	High school
Jimi Hocking	U.S. singer–songwriter	High school
Billie Holiday	U.S. jazz singer	Elementary school
John Lee Hooker	U.S. singer–songwriter	High school
Fiona Horne	Australian singer	High school
Lena Horne	U.S. singer	High school
Janis Ian	U.S. singer–songwriter	High school
Enrique Iglesias	Spanish singer	College
Natalie Imbruglia	Australian singer, actress	High school
Burl Ives	U.S. folk singer	College
LL Cool J	Rap artist	High school
Waylon Jennings	U.S. singer, guitarist	High school
Joan Jett	U.S. singer, guitarist	High school
Billy Joel	U.S. singer–songwriter, pianist	High school
George Jones	U.S. country singer	Elementary school
Norah Jones	U.S. singer–songwriter, pianist	College
Rickie Lee Jones	U.S. singer–songwriter	High school
Tom Jones	Welsh pop singer	High school
Joshua Kadison	U.S. rock pianist–composer	High school
Chaka Khan	U.S. singer	High school
B.B. King	U.S. singer–songwriter, blues guitarist	High school
Gladys Knight	U.S. singer, actress	High school
J. Fred Knobloch	U.S. singer–songwriter	High school
Cleo Laine	U.K. jazz singer	High school
Cyndi Lauper	U.S. pop singer, actress	High school
Avril Lavigne	Canadian singer–songwriter, actress	High school
Steve Lawrence	U.S. singer, actor	High school
Albert Lee	U.K. guitarist	High school
Sean Lennon	U.S. musician	College
Huey Lewis	U.S. singer, musician	College
Jerry Lee Lewis	U.S. singer–songwriter, pianist	High school
Mark Lindsay	Paul Revere and the Raiders lead singer	High school
Brian Littrell	U.S. singer, member of Backstreet Boys	High school
David Lon	U.S. musician	High school
Julie London	U.S. singer, actress	High school
Trini Lopez	U.S. singer, guitarist	High school
Courtney Love	U.S. singer, actress	High school
Loretta Lynn	U.S. country singer	High school
Shelby Lynne	U.S. singer–songwriter	High school
Madonna	U.S. singer–songwriter, actress, author	College
Shirley Manson	Scottish musician, singer	High school
Dean Martin	U.S. singer, actor	High school
John Mayer	U.S. singer–songwriter	College
Natalie Merchant	U.S. singer–songwriter	High school

Appendix

Name	Reminder	Dropped Out
\multicolumn{3}{c}{The Performing Arts (continued)}		
\multicolumn{3}{c}{Musicians and Singers (continued)}		
George Michael	U.K. singer–songwriter	High school
Roger Miller	U.S. singer–songwriter	Elementary school
Steve Miller	U.S. guitarist	College
Liza Minnelli	U.S. singer, actress	High school
Bill Monroe	U.S. singer, composer, bandleader	Elementary school
John Michael Montgomery	U.S. country singer	High school
John Mooney	U.S. blues guitarist	High school
Van Morrison	Irish singer–songwriter	High school
Samantha Mumba	Irish pop singer, actress	High school
Nelly	Rap artist	High school
Willie Nelson	U.S. singer–songwriter	College
Wayne Newton	U.S. pop singer	High school
Olivia Newton-John	Australian singer, actress	High school
Sinéad O'Connor	Irish singer–songwriter	High school
Gil Ofarim	German singer–songwriter, actor	High school
Kelly Osbourne	U.K. singer, actress, fashion designer	High school
Ozzy Osbourne	U.K. singer	High school
Jimmy Page	U.K. rock guitarist	High school
Charlie Parker	U.S. jazz saxophonist	High school
Neil Peart	Canadian drummer, lyricist	High school
Tom Petty	U.S. singer–songwriter	High school
Pink	U.S. singer–songwriter	High school
Charley Pride	U.S. country singer	High school
Prince	U.S. singer–songwriter	High school
Otis Redding	U.S. singer	High school
Lou Reed	U.S. singer–songwriter	College
J.J. Reneaux	U.S. singer–songwriter, author	High school
Paul Revere	U.S. rock organist	High school
Trent Reznor	U.S. singer–songwriter	College
Charlie Rich	U.S. blues singer	College
Busta Rhymes	Rap artist	High school
Kid Rock	Rap artist	High school
Axl Rose	U.S. singer–songwriter	High school
Ja Rule	Rap artist	High school
Seal	U.K. soul singer	High school
Pete Seeger	U.S. folk singer	College
Frank Sinatra	U.S. pop singer	High school
Sammi Smith	U.S. country singer	High school
Scott Stapp	U.S. singer–songwriter	High school
Ringo Starr	U.K. rock drummer, singer	High school
Donna Summer	U.S. pop singer	High school
James Taylor	U.S. singer–songwriter	High school
Koko Taylor	U.S. blues singer	Elementary school
Rob Thomas	U.S. pop singer	High school
Cyndi Thomson	U.S. country singer	College
Jeff Timmons	U.S. pop singer	College
Randy Travis	U.S. country singer	High school

Millionaire Dropouts

Name	Reminder	Dropped Out
\multicolumn{3}{c}{*The Performing Arts (continued)*}		
\multicolumn{3}{c}{*Musicians and Singers (continued)*}		
Robin Trower	U.K. rock guitarist	High school
Tanya Tucker	U.S. country singer	High school
Steven Tyler	U.S. singer–songwriter	High school
Stevie Ray Vaughan	U.S. blues guitarist	High school
Eddie Vedder	U.S. singer	High school
Sid Vicious	U.K. rock musician	High school
Eddie Walker	U.K. singer–songwriter	High school
Steve Waller	U.K. singer, guitarist	High school
Doc Watson	U.S. singer–songwriter	Elementary school
Kitty Wells	U.S. country singer	High school
Kanye West	Rap artist	College
Barry White	U.S. pop singer, record producer	High school
Hank Williams	U.S. singer–songwriter	High school
Lucinda Williams	U.S. singer–songwriter	High school
Eric Wright	Rap artist	High school
Tammy Wynette	U.S. singer–songwriter	High school
Neil Young	Canadian singer–songwriter	High school
\multicolumn{3}{c}{*Comedians*}		
Cliff Arquette	Created the character Charley Weaver	High school
Roseanne Barr	*Roseanne Bar Show*	High school
Jack Benny	Vaudeville, radio, early television	High school
Joey Bishop	Comedy writer, straight man	High school
Carol Burnett	*Carol Burnett Show*	College
George Burns	Vaudeville, radio, television	High school
Eddie Cantor	Vaudeville, television	Elementary school
George Carlin	Standup, television	High school
Billy Connolly	Scottish standup and sketch comic	High school
Bill Cosby	Standup; *I Spy, The Cosby Show*	High school
Ellen DeGeneres	Standup; *Ellen*	College
Redd Foxx	Standup; *Sanford and Son*	High school
Jackie Gleason	*The Honeymooners*	High school
Whoopi Goldberg	Standup, television, film	High school
Benny Hill	*Benny Hill Show*	High school
D.L. Hughley	Standup, television	High school
Kevin James	*The King of Queens*	College
Alan King	Standup, television, film	High school
George Kirby	*The George Kirby Show*	High school
Jerry Lewis	Slapstick standup, film, television	High school
Groucho Marx	Marx Brothers	Elementary school
Rosie O'Donnell	Standup, television, film	College
Paula Poundstone	Comedy writer, standup, television	High school
Richard Pryor	Standup, television, film	High school
Gilda Radner	*Saturday Night Live*	College
Chris Rock	Standup, film	High school
Red Skelton	Vaudeville, stage, radio, television, film	Elementary school
Tracey Ullman	*The Tracey Ullman Show*	High school

www.MillionaireDropouts.com

Appendix

Name	Reminder	Dropped Out
\multicolumn{3}{c}{The Performing Arts (*continued*)}		

The Performing Arts (*continued*)
Comedians (*continued*)

Name	Reminder	Dropped Out
Damon Wayans	Wayans Brothers Productions	High school
Keenan Ivory Wayans	Wayans Brothers Productions	College
Marlon Wayans	Wayans Brothers Productions	College
Flip Wilson	*The Flip Wilson Show*	High school
Ernie Wise	U.K. television comic, *Morecambe and Wise*	High school

Illusionists

Name	Reminder	Dropped Out
David Copperfield	Made the Statue of Liberty disappear	College
Harry Houdini	Escape artist	High school
James Randi	Escape artist	High school
Howard Thurston	Entertained over 60 million people before 1932	Elementary school

Actors

Name	Reminder	Dropped Out
Don Adams	*Get Smart*	High school
Danny Aiello	*Moonstruck*	High school
Jack Albertson	*Days of Wine and Roses*	High school
Anthony Andrews	*Haunted*	High school
Dan Aykroyd	*Ghostbusters*	College
Lew Ayres	*Of Mice and Men*	College
Kevin Bacon	*Mystic River, Footloose*	High school
Sean Bean	*National Treasure*	High school
Warren Beatty	*Bonnie and Clyde, Dick Tracy*	College
Jean-Paul Belmondo	*Hold-Up, Les Misérables*	High school
Orlando Bloom	*The Lord of the Rings*	High school
Humphrey Bogart	*Casablanca*	High school
Marlon Brando	*A Streetcar Named Desire, The Godfather*	High school
Charles Bronson	*Death Wish*	High school
Pierce Brosnan	*The Thomas Crown Affair*	High school
Raymond Burr	*Perry Mason*	High school
James Caan	*The Godfather*	High school
Sebastian Cabot	*Family Affair*	High school
Nicolas Cage	*Leaving Las Vegas, Gone in Sixty Seconds*	High school
James Cagney	*Yankee Doodle Dandy, Mr. Roberts, Ragtime*	College
Michael Caine	*Alfie, The Man Who Would Be King*	High school
Keith Carradine	*Nashville, Will Rogers Follies, Deadwood*	College
Jim Carrey	*Ace Ventura Pet Detective, Liar Liar*	High school
Charlie Chaplin	*Modern Times*	Elementary school
Maurice Chevalier	*Gigi*	High school
Sean Connery	*Goldfinger, The Rock, The Avengers*	High school
Noel Coward	*Around the World in 80 Days, The Italian Job*	Elementary school
Michael Crawford	*Phantom of the Opera*	High school
Russell Crowe	*Gladiator*	High school
Tom Cruise	*Mission Impossible*	High school
Matt Damon	*Good Will Hunting*	College
Jeff Daniels	*Dumb and Dumber*	College
Robert De Niro	*Taxi Driver, Raging Bull, Analyze This*	High school
James Dean	*Rebel without a Cause*	College
Reginald Denny	*Batman*	High school

Millionaire Dropouts

Name	Reminder	Dropped Out
\multicolumn{3}{c}{The Performing Arts (continued)}		
\multicolumn{3}{c}{Actors (continued)}		
Gerard Depardieu	Green Card, The Man in the Iron Mask	Elementary school
Johnny Depp	Edward Scissorhands, Pirates of the Caribbean	High school
Leonardo Di Caprio	Titanic	High school
Vin Diesel	Saving Private Ryan, XXX	College
Matt Dillon	The Flamingo Kid, There's Something about Mary	High school
Brad Dourif	The Lord of The Rings	College
Robert Downey Jr.	Chaplin; Good Night, and Good Luck.	High school
Charles Durning	O Brother, Where Art Thou	High school
Rupert Everett	My Best Friend's Wedding	High school
Peter Facinelli	The Scorpion King	College
Colin Farrell	Daredevil	High school
Errol Flynn	Captain Blood, The Adventures of Robin Hood	High school
Ben Foster	The Laramie Project, Hostage	High school
Michael J. Fox	Back to the Future	High school
Jamie Foxx	Ray	College
Clark Gable	Gone with the Wind	High school
James Garner	Maverick, The Rockford Files, The Great Escape	High school
Richard Gere	Pretty Woman	College
Topher Grace	That 70's Show	College
Cary Grant	She Done Him Wrong, To Catch a Thief, Charade	High school
Gene Hackman	Bonnie and Clyde, The Birdcage, Heist	High school
Tom Hanks	Forrest Gump	College
Ethan Hawke	Training Day	College
Sterling Hayden	Dr. Strangelove	High school
Dustin Hoffman	The Graduate, Tootsie, Rain Man	College
Paul Hogan	Crocodile Dundee	High school
Bob Hope	Road to Rio, The Seven Little Foys, Spies Like Us	High school
Bob Hoskins	Enemy of the State	High school
Djimon Hounsou	Gladiator	College
Joshua Jackson	Dawson Creek	High school
Michael Keaton	Beetlejuice, Batman	College
Harvey Keitel	Thelma and Louise, Pulp Fiction	High school
Chris Klein	American Pie	College
Yaphet Kotto	Homicide	High school
Ashton Kutcher	That 70's Show	College
Jude Law	The Talented Mr. Ripley, The Aviator	High school
Heath Ledger	Brokeback Mountain	High school
Jason Lee	Chasing Amy, Mallrats	High school
Jarod Leto	Panic Room	High school
Tobey Maguire	Spider-Man	High school
Evan Marriot	Joe Millionaire	High school
Steve Martin	The Jerk, Roxanne, Shopgirl	College
Lee Marvin	Cat Ballou, The Dirty Dozen, M Squad	High school
Ewan McGregor	Star Wars	High school
Steve McQueen	The Great Escape	High school
Robert Mitchum	Cape Fear	High school
Yves Montand	Z; On a Clear Day, You Can See Forever	Elementary school

Appendix

Name	Reminder	Dropped Out
The Performing Arts (continued)		
Actors (continued)		
Roger Moore	Live and Let Die, For Your Eyes Only	High school
Donny Most	Happy Days	College
Bill Murray	Groundhog Day, Ed Wood, Lost in Translation	College
Dustin Nguyen	21 Jump Street	College
Peter O'Toole	Lawrence of Arabia	High school
Al Pacino	The Godfather	High school
Joe Pesci	Goodfellas	High school
Joaquin Phoenix	Gladiator	High school
Brad Pitt	A River Runs Through It, Mr. and Mrs. Smith	College
Donald Pleasance	Halloween	High school
Sidney Poitier	A Raisin in the Sun, In the Heat of the Night, Jackal	Elementary school
Dennis Quaid	Any Given Sunday	College
Anthony Quinn	Zorba the Greek, The Guns of Navarone	High school
Anthony Rapp	Rent	College
Keanu Reeves	Matrix	High school
Burt Reynolds	Smokey and the Bandit	College
Roy Rogers	The Roy Rogers Show	High school
Charlie Sheen	Platoon, Hot Shots, Two and a Half Men	High school
Christian Slater	Broken Arrow, The Contender, Alone in the Dark	High school
Kevin Sorbo	Hercules	College
Kevin Spacey	L.A. Confidential, American Beauty, K-PAX	High school
Sylvester Stallone	Rocky	College
Rod Steiger	The Pawnbroker, Doctor Zhivago	High school
Patrick Stewart	Dune, Lady Jane, L.A. Story	High school
Eric Stoltz	Fast Times at Ridgemont High	High school
Danny Thomas	The Danny Thomas Show	High school
John Travolta	Saturday Night Fever, Grease, Pulp Fiction	High school
Peter Ustinov	Spartacus, Topkapi, Alice in Wonderland	High school
Jean-Claude Van Damme	Time Cop	High school
Ken Wahl	Wise Guy	High school
Mark Wahlberg	Boogie Nights, Four Brothers	High school
Clint Walker	Dirty Dozen	High school
Bruce Willis	Die Hard	College
Anson Wilson	Happy Days	College
Owen Wilson	Meet the Parents, Wedding Crashers	High school
Paul Winfield	Terminator	College
Elijah Wood	Lord of the Rings	High school
James Woods	Casino	College
Actresses		
Julie Andrews	My Fair Lady, Mary Poppins, The Sound of Music	High school
Christina Applegate	Married…with Children	High school
Courtney Cox Arquette	Friends	College
Lucille Ball	I Love Lucy	High school
Brigitte Bardot	And God Created Woman, Helen of Troy	High school
Drew Barrymore	E.T., Scream, Riding in Cars with Boys	High school
Kate Beckinsale	Pearl Harbor	College

Millionaire Dropouts

Name	Reminder	Dropped Out
\multicolumn{3}{c}{The Performing Arts (continued)}		
\multicolumn{3}{c}{Actresses (continued)}		
Karen Black	Five Easy Pieces	High school
Clara Bow	Wings	High school
Louise Brooks	The Canary Murder Case	High school
Ellen Burstyn	The Last Picture Show; Same Time, Next Year	High school
Neve Campbell	Scream	High school
Jill Clayburgh	An Unmarried Woman	College
Toni Collette	The Sixth Sense	High school
Joan Crawford	What Ever Happened to Baby Jane?	High school
Beverly D'Angelo	Vegas Vacation	High school
Majandra Delfino	Traffic	High school
Bo Derek	10, Bolero	High school
Cameron Diaz	There's Something About Mary, Charlie's Angels	High school
Patty Duke	The Miracle Worker	High school
Jeanne Eagels	Jealousy	High school
Carrie Fisher	Star Wars, The Blues Brothers, When Harry Met Sally	High school
Tara Fitzgerald	Like Father Like Son	College
Eva Gabor	Gigi	High school
Greta Garbo	Grand Hotel, Anna Karenina, Ninotchka	High school
Jennie Garth	Beverly Hills 90210	High school
Lillian Gish	Miss Susie Slagle's, The Unforgiven	College
Susan Hampshire	The Forsyte Saga, The Grand	High school
Margaux Hemingway	Lipstick, Dangerous Cargo	High school
Helen Hunt	As Good As It Gets	College
Iman	L.A. Story	High school
Angelina Jolie	Girl, Interrupted; Gone in Sixty Seconds	High school
Nicole Kidman	Eyes Wide Shut, Moulin Rouge!, Cold Mountain	High school
Eartha Kitt	St. Louis Blues, Batman, Fatal Instinct	High school
Jennifer Jason Leigh	Fast Times at Ridgemont High	High school
Juliette Lewis	Natural Born Killers	High school
Heather Locklear	Spin City	College
Traci Lords	Growing Pains	High school
Sophia Loren	Desire Under the Elms, Two Women	Elementary school
Andie MacDowell	Groundhog Day, Multiplicity	College
Jena Malone	Cold Mountain	High school
Sophie Marceau	The World Is Not Enough	High school
Vanessa Marcil	Las Vegas	High school
Kelly McGillis	Top Gun	High school
Eva Mendes	Hitch	College
Alyssa Milano	Charmed	High school
Tina Modotti	The Tiger's Coat	Elementary school
Marilyn Monroe	The Seven Year Itch, The Misfits	High school
Demi Moore	Ghost, Disclosure	High school
Meg Mullally	Will and Grace	College
Julie Newmar	Seven Brides For Seven Brothers	College
Cathy Podewell	Dallas	College
Sarah Polley	Dawn Of The Dead	High school
Teri Polo	Meet the Fockers	High school

Appendix

Name	Reminder	Dropped Out
\multicolumn{3}{c}{*The Performing Arts (continued)*}		

The Performing Arts (continued)

Actresses (continued)

Name	Reminder	Dropped Out
Leah Remini	*The King of Queens*	High school
Michelle Rodriguez	*S.W.A.T.*	High school
Theresa Russell	*Black Widow*	High school
Rene Russo	*Tin Cup, The Thomas Crown Affair*	High school
Roselyn Sanchez	*Rush Hour 2*	College
Catya Sassoon	*Inside Out*	High school
Alicia Silverstone	*Clueless*	High school
Sharon Stone	*Basic Instinct, Casino*	College
Hilary Swank	*Million Dollar Baby*	High school
Uma Thurman	*Kill Bill*	High school
Marisa Tomei	*My Cousin Vinny*	College
Twiggy	*The Blues Brothers*	High school
Susan Ward	*Shallow Hal*	High school
Estella Warren	*Driven*	High school
Naomi Watts	*Mulholland Drive, The Ring*	High school
Mae West	*She Done Him Wrong, My Little Chickadee*	High school
Kate Winslet	*Titanic*	High school
Catherine Zeta-Jones	*Chicago*	High school

Sports

Team Sports

Name	Reminder	Dropped Out
Willy Aybar	Los Angels Dodgers	High school
Yogi Berra	Yankees	High school
Roberto Clemente	Pittsburgh Pirates	High school
Joe DiMaggio	New York Yankees	High school
Miura Kazuyoshi	Soccer player, Japanese National Team	High school
Tommy Lasorda	Baseball team manager	High school
Tommy Nunez	Basketball referee	High school
Bobby Orr	Boston Bruins	High school
William Owens	NLBPA–Memphis	Elementary school
Pelé	Brazilian soccer player	Elementary school
Joe Pepitone	New York Yankees	High school
Manny Ramirez	Boston Red Sox	High school
Derek Sanderson	New York Rangers	High school
Sammy Sosa	Baltimore Orioles	High school
Casey Stengel	New York Mets	High school
Miguel Tejada	Oakland Athletics	High school
Fernando Valenzuela	St. Louis Cardinals	High school

Individual Sports

Name	Reminder	Dropped Out
Mario Andretti	Race car driver	Elementary school
Boris Becker	Tennis player	High school
Bjorn Borg	Tennis player	High school
Jennifer Capriati	Tennis player	High school
Dale Earnhardt	Stock car driver	High school
Nick Faldo	Golfer	High school

MILLIONAIRE DROPOUTS

Name	Reminder	Dropped Out
Sports (continued)		
Individual Sports (continued)		
Gigi Fernández	Tennis player	College
Scott Fischer	Climber	High school
George Foreman	Boxer	High school
A.J. Foyt	Race car driver	High school
Joe Frazier	Boxer	High school
Laird Hamilton	Surfer	High school
Thomas Hearns	Boxer	High school
Larry Holmes	Boxer	Elementary school
David L. Jackson	Boxer	High school
Tony Jacklin	Golfer	High school
Jean-Claude Killy	Skier	High school
Rod Laver	Tennis player	High school
Joe Louis	Boxer	High school
Brian Orser	Ice skater	High school
Floyd Patterson	Boxer,	High school
Mary Lou Retton	Gymnast	High school
Chi Chi Rodriguez	Golfer	High school
Paul P-Rod Rodriguez	Skateboarder	High school
Gene Sarazen	Golfer	Elementary school
Willie Shoemaker	Jockey	High school
Jackie Stewart	Race car driver	High school
Alberto Tomba	Skier	High school
Lee Trevino	Golfer	High school
Ron Turcotte	Jockey	High school
Ian Woosnam	Golfer	High school
Mildred "Babe" Zaharias	Olympic gold medalist, star of multiple sports	High school

Give the gift of Millionaire Dropouts™ to your friends, family and business associates

Order here and we will ship for free

- ☐ YES, I want _____ copies of *Millionaire Dropouts: Inspiring Stories of the World's Most Successful Failures* at $16.95 each.

- ☐ YES, I want _____ copies of *Millionaire Dropouts High School Edition: Never Let Your Schooling Interfere with Your Education* at $12.95 each.

- ☐ YES, I want _____ copies of *Millionaire Dropouts College Edition: Why Dropping Out Might Be the Best Decision You Ever Made* at $14.95 each.

- ☐ YES, I want _____ copies of *Millionaire Dropouts Parents Edition: Why You Should Support Your Child Who Wants to Drop Out* at $16.95 each.

- ☐ YES, I want _____ copies of *Millionaire Dropouts Biography Edition: Biographies of the World's Most Successful Failures* at $16.95 each.

- ☐ YES, I want _____ copies of *Millionaire Dropouts Mini-Book: Words of Wisdom* at $6.95 each.

- ☐ YES, I want _____ copies of *Millionaire Dropouts Mini-Book: Innovators* at $6.95 each.

- ☐ YES, I want to receive my FREE subscription to Millionaire Dropouts electronic monthly newsletter. My email address is listed below.

- ☐ YES, I am interested in having Woody Woodward speak to my organization. Please contact me with details.

Please charge my:
☐ Visa ☐ Master Card ☐ American Express ☐ Discover

Credit card number _____

Expiration date (month/year) _____/_____

Name _____

Organization _____

Title _____

Address _____

_____

City _____ State _____ Zip _____

Phone _____ Fax _____

Email (please print clearly) _____

Signature _____

Privacy Policy: We hate junk mail as much as you therefore we don't send any.

Three ways to order

1. Return completed form to:

    D.U. Publishing
    39252 Winchester Road #107-430
    Murrieta CA 92563

2. Order online at www.MillionaireDropouts.com

3. Fax orders to 951-346-3280